SAMS
Teach
Yourself

PHP

Chris Newman

in 10 Minutes

SAMS   800 East 96th Street, Indianapolis, Indiana, 46240 USA

Sams Teach Yourself PHP in 10 Minutes

Copyright © 2005 by Sams Publishing

International Standard Book Number: 0-672-32762-7

Library of Congress Catalog Card Number: 2004098028

Printed in the United States of America

First Printing: April 2005

08   07   4   3

Trademarks

All terms mentioned in this book that are known to be trademarks or service marks have been appropriately capitalized. Sams Publishing cannot attest to the accuracy of this information. Use of a term in this book should not be regarded as affecting the validity of any trademark or service mark.

Warning and Disclaimer

Every effort has been made to make this book as complete and as accurate as possible, but no warranty or fitness is implied. The information provided is on an "as is" basis. The author and the publisher shall have neither liability nor responsibility to any person or entity with respect to any loss or damages arising from the information contained in this book.

Bulk Sales

Sams Publishing offers excellent discounts on this book when ordered in quantity for bulk purchases or special sales. For more information, please contact

U.S. Corporate and Government Sales
1-800-382-3419
corpsales@pearsontechgroup.com

For sales outside of the U.S., please contact

International Sales
international@pearsoned.com

ACQUISITIONS EDITOR
Shelley Johnston

DEVELOPMENT EDITOR
Damon Jordan

MANAGING EDITOR
Charlotte Clapp

SENIOR PROJECT EDITOR
Matthew Purcell

COPY EDITOR
Kitty Jarrett

INDEXER
Chris Barrick

PROOFREADER
Paula Lowell

TECHNICAL EDITOR
Sara Goleman

PUBLISHING COORDINATOR
Vanessa Evans

INTERIOR DESIGNER
Gary Adair

COVER DESIGNER
Aren Howell

PAGE LAYOUT
Susan Geiselman

Contents

PART III   The Web Environment

PART IV   Using Other Services from PHP

PART **VI**   Appendix

About the Author

Chris Newman is a consultant programmer specializing in the development of custom web-based database applications to a loyal international client base.

A graduate of Keele University, Chris lives in Stoke-on-Trent, England, where he runs Lightwood Consultancy Ltd., the company he founded in 1999 to further his interest in Internet technology. Lightwood operates web hosting services under the DataSnake brand and is proud to be one of the first hosting companies to offer and support SQLite in addition to PHP as a standard feature on all accounts.

More information on Lightwood Consultancy Ltd. can be found at www.lightwood.net, and Chris can be contacted at chris@lightwood.net.

We Want to Hear from You!

As the reader of this book, *you* are our most important critic and commentator. We value your opinion and want to know what we're doing right, what we could do better, what areas you'd like to see us publish in, and any other words of wisdom you're willing to pass our way.

You can email or write me directly to let me know what you did or didn't like about this book—as well as what we can do to make our books stronger.

Please note that I cannot help you with technical problems related to the topic of this book, and that due to the high volume of mail I receive, I might not be able to reply to every message.

When you write, please be sure to include this book's title and author as well as your name and phone or email address. I will carefully review your comments and share them with the author and editors who worked on the book.

Email: opensource@samspublishing.com

Mail: Mark Taber
           Associate Publisher
           Sams Publishing
           800 East 96th Street
           Indianapolis, IN 46240 USA

Reader Services

For more information about this book or another Sams Publishing title, visit our Web site, at www.samspublishing.com. Type the ISBN (excluding hyphens) or the title of a book in the Search field to find the page you're looking for.

Introduction: Welcome to PHP

This book is about PHP, one of the most popular web scripting languages around. It is a book for busy people. Each lesson takes just 10 minutes to work through, so if you have wanted to learn PHP for a while but have never really had the chance, don't put it off any longer!

Who This Book Is For

This book is aimed at those who want to learn PHP, even if they don't have any previous programming or scripting experience. You can even use this book to learn PHP as a first programming language if you do not have any previous experience.

If you have some previous programming experience but have not written for the web before, you can use this book to learn about the PHP language and how to apply programming techniques to the web environment.

This book does not teach you HTML. Although knowledge of HTML is not a prerequisite, having published web pages in the past will be an advantage—even if you do not usually hand-code HTML.

How This Book Is Organized

This book is organized into five parts.

Part I: PHP Foundations

The lessons in Part I introduce the basic building blocks of the PHP language.

- **Lesson 1: Getting to Know PHP.** This chapter introduces you to what PHP is all about and gives some simple examples to show how PHP is used inside a web page.

- **Lesson 2: Variables.** This chapter explains how you assign values to variables and demonstrates some simple expressions.

- **Lesson 3: Flow Control.** This chapter examines the conditional and looping constructs that allow you to control the flow of a PHP script.

- **Lesson 4: Functions.** This chapter explains how you can modularize and reuse a frequently used section of code as a function.

Part II: Working with Data

The lessons in Part II examine in more detail the different types of data that can be manipulated by PHP:

- **Lesson 5: Working with Numbers.** This chapter gives more detailed examples of the numeric manipulation you can perform in PHP.

- **Lesson 6: Working with Strings.** This chapter examines the powerful set of string functions that PHP provides.

- **Lesson 7: Working with Arrays.** This chapter explains how arrays work and examines the PHP functions that can manipulate this powerful data type.

- **Lesson 8: Regular Expressions.** This chapter shows how to perform complex string manipulation by using powerful regular expressions.

- **Lesson 9: Working with Dates and Times.** This chapter examines how to use date and time values in a PHP script.

- **Lesson 10: Using Classes.** This chapter introduces you to object-oriented PHP and examines how you define and access a class in a script.

Part III: The Web Environment

The lessons in Part III deal with using PHP specifically in the web environment:

- **Lesson 11: Processing HTML Forms.** This chapter shows how you use PHP to process user-submitted input from an HTML form.

- **Lesson 12: Generating Dynamic HTML.** This chapter examines some techniques for creating HTML components on-the-fly from PHP.

- **Lesson 13: Form Validation.** This chapter examines some techniques for validating user-submitted input from an HTML form.

- **Lesson 14: Cookies and Sessions.** This chapter shows how to pass data between pages by using PHP sessions and how to send cookies to a user's browser.

- **Lesson 15: User Authentication.** This chapter examines some techniques for validating user-submitted input from an HTML form.

- **Lesson 16: Communicating with the Web Server.** This chapter looks at ways in which PHP can interact with a web server.

Part IV: Using Other Services from PHP

Part IV looks at how PHP can communicate with external programs and services:

- **Lesson 17: Filesystem Access.** This chapter examines the PHP functions that enable you to access the filesystem.

- **Lesson 18: Host Program Execution.** This chapter examines the PHP functions that enable you to execute programs on the host system.

- **Lesson 19: Using a MySQL Database.** This chapter shows how to use a MySQL database for data storage and retrieval from PHP.

- **Lesson 20: Database Abstraction.** This chapter explains how you can access a database through an abstraction layer to make scripts more portable.

- **Lesson 21: Running PHP on the Command Line.** This chapter shows how you can use PHP as a powerful shell scripting language.

- **Lesson 22: Error Handling and Debugging.** This chapter discusses some techniques for finding and fixing bugs in scripts.

Part V: Configuring and Extending PHP

The final part of the book deals with PHP administration:

- **Lesson 23: PHP Configuration.** This chapter explains some of the popular configuration options that can be set at runtime to change the behavior of PHP.

- **Lesson 24: PHP Security.** This chapter discusses security issues in PHP scripts and shows how you can use Safe Mode on a shared web server.

- **Lesson 25: Using PEAR.** This chapter introduces the freely available classes that are available in the PHP Extension and Application Repository.

Versions of Software Covered

At the time of writing, the current version of PHP is PHP 5.0.3. Unless otherwise stated, all code examples in this book will work with PHP 4.1.0 and higher.

Conventions Used in This Book

This book uses different typefaces to differentiate between code and regular English, and also to help you identify important concepts.

Text that you type and text that should appear on your screen is presented in monospace type.

```
It will look like this to mimic the way text looks on your
screen.
```

Placeholders for variables and expressions appear in *monospace italic* font. You should replace the placeholder with the specific value it represents.

A Note presents interesting pieces of information related to the surrounding discussion.

A Tip offers advice or teaches an easier way to do something.

A Caution advises you about potential problems and helps you steer clear of disaster.

LESSON 1

Getting to Know PHP

In this lesson you will find out what PHP is all about and see what it is able to do.

PHP Basics

There is a good chance you already know a bit about what PHP can do—that is probably why you have picked up this book. PHP is hugely popular, and rightly so. Even if you haven't come across an existing user singing its praises, you've almost certainly used a website that runs on PHP. This lesson clarifies what PHP does, how it works, and what it is capable of.

PHP is a programming language that was designed for creating dynamic websites. It slots into your web server and processes instructions contained in a web page before that page is sent through to your web browser. Certain elements of the page can therefore be generated on-the-fly so that the page changes each time it is loaded. For instance, you can use PHP to show the current date and time at the top of each page in your site, as you'll see later in this lesson.

The name PHP is a recursive acronym that stands for *PHP: Hypertext Preprocessor*. It began life called PHP/FI, the "FI" part standing for *Forms Interpreter*. Though the name was shortened a while back, one of PHP's most powerful features is how easy it becomes to process data submitted in HTML forms. PHP can also talk to various database systems, giving you the ability to generate a web page based on a SQL query.

For example, you could enter a search keyword into a form field on a web page, query a database with this value, and produce a page of matching results. You will have seen this kind of application many times before, at virtually any online store as well as many websites that do not sell anything, such as search engines.

The PHP language is flexible and fairly forgiving, making it easy to learn even if you have not done any programming in the past. If you already know another language, you will almost certainly find similarities here. PHP looks like a cross between C, Perl, and Java, and if you are familiar with any of these, you will find that you can adapt your existing programming style to PHP with little effort.

Server-Side Scripting

The most important concept to learn when starting out with PHP is where exactly it fits into the grand scheme of things in a web environment. When you understand this, you will understand what PHP can and cannot do.

The PHP module attaches to your web server, telling it that files with a particular extension should be examined for PHP code. Any PHP code found in the page is executed—with any PHP code replaced by the output it produces—before the web page is sent to the browser.

> **File Extensions**   The usual web server configuration is that `somefile.php` will be interpreted by PHP, whereas `somefile.html` will be passed straight through to the web browser, without PHP getting involved.

The only time the PHP interpreter is called upon to do something is when a web page is loaded. This could be when you click a link, submit a form, or just type in the URL of a web page. When the web browser has finished downloading the page, PHP plays no further part until your browser requests another page.

Because it is only possible to check the values entered in an HTML form when the submit button is clicked, PHP cannot be used to perform client-side validation—in other words, to check that the value entered in one field meets certain criteria before allowing you to proceed to the next field. Client-side validation can be done using JavaScript, a language that runs inside the web browser itself, and JavaScript and PHP can be used together if that is the effect you require.

The beauty of PHP is that it does not rely on the web browser at all; your script will run the same way whatever browser you use. When writing server-side code, you do not need to worry about JavaScript being enabled or about compatibility with older browsers beyond the ability to display HTML that your script generates or is embedded in.

PHP Tags

Consider the following extract from a PHP-driven web page that displays the current date:

```
Today is <?php echo date('j F Y');?>
```

The `<?php` tag tells PHP that everything that follows is program code rather than HTML, until the closing `?>` tag. In this example, the `echo` command tells PHP to display the next item to screen; the following `date` command produces a formatted version of the current date, containing the day, month, and year.

> **The Statement Terminator**   The semicolon character is used to indicate the end of a PHP command. In the previous examples, there is only one command, and the semicolon is not actually required, but it is good practice to always include it to show that a command is complete.

In this book PHP code appears inside tags that look like `<?php ... ?>`. Other tag styles can be used, so you may come across other people's PHP code beginning with tags that look like `<?` (the short tag), `<%` (the ASP tag style) or `<SCRIPT LANGUAGE="php">` (the script tag).

Of the different tag styles that can be used, only the full <?php tag and the script tag are always available. The others are turned off or on by using a PHP configuration setting. We will look at the php.ini configuration file in Lesson 23, "PHP Configuration."

> **Standard PHP Tags**   It is good practice to always use the <?php tag style so your code will run on any system that has PHP installed, with no additional configuration needed. If you are tempted to use <? as a short-cut, know that any time you move your code to another web server, you need to be sure it will understand this tag style.

Anything that is not enclosed in PHP tags is passed straight through to the browser, exactly as it appears in the script. Therefore, in the previous example, the text Today is appears before the generated date when the page is displayed.

Your First Script

Before you go any further, you need to make sure you can create and run PHP scripts as you go through the examples in this book. This could be on your own machine, and you can find instructions for installing PHP in Appendix A, "Installing PHP." Also, many web hosting companies include PHP in their packages, and you may already have access to a suitable piece of web space.

Go ahead and create a new file called time.php that contains Listing 1.1, in a location that can be accessed by a PHP-enabled web server. This is a slight variation on the date example shown previously.

LISTING 1.1   Displaying the System Date and Time

```
The time is
<?php echo date('H:i:s');?>
and the date is
<?php echo date('j F Y');?>
```

When you enter the URL to this file in your web browser, you should see the current date and time, according to the system clock on your web server, displayed.

> **Running PHP Locally**   If you are running PHP from your local PC, PHP code in a script will be executed only if it is accessed through a web server that has the PHP module enabled. If you open a local script directly in the web browser—for instance, by double-clicking or dragging and dropping the file into the browser—it will be treated as HTML only.

> **Web Document Location**   If you were using a default Apache installation in Windows, you would create `time.php` in the folder `C:\Program Files\Apache Group\Apache\htdocs`, and the correct URL would be http://localhost/time.php.

If you entered Listing 1.1 exactly as shown, you might notice that the actual output produced could be formatted a little better—there is no space between the time and the word *and*. Any line in a script that only contains code inside PHP tags will not take up a line of output in the generated HTML.

If you use the View Source option in your web browser, you can see the exact output produced by your script, which should look similar to the following:

```
The time is
15:33:09and the date is
13 October 2004
```

If you insert a space character after ?>, that line now contains non-PHP elements, and the output is spaced correctly.

The echo Command

While PHP is great for embedding small, dynamic elements inside a web page, in fact the whole page could consist of a set of PHP instructions to generate the output if the entire script were enclosed in PHP tags.

The echo command is used to send output to the browser. Listing 1.1 uses echo to display the result of the date command, which returns a string that contains a formatted version of the current date. Listing 1.2 does the same thing but uses a series of echo commands in a single block of PHP code to display the date and time.

LISTING 1.2   Using echo to Send Output to the Browser

```php
<?php
echo "The time is ";
echo date('H:i:s');
echo " and the date is ";
echo date('j F Y');
?>
```

The non-dynamic text elements you want to output are contained in quotation marks. Either double quotes (as used in Listing 1.2) or single quotes (the same character used for an apostrophe) can be used to enclose text strings, although you will see an important difference between the two styles in Lesson 2, "Variables." The following statements are equally valid:

```php
echo "The time is ";
echo 'The time is ';
```

Notice that space characters are used in these statements inside the quotation marks to ensure that the output from date is spaced away from the surrounding text. In fact the output from Listing 1.2 is slightly different from that for Listing 1.1, but in a web browser you will need to use View Source to see the difference. The raw output from Listing 1.2 is as follows:

```
The time is 15:59:50 and the date is 13 October 2004
```

There are no line breaks in the page source produced this time. In a web browser, the output looks just the same as for Listing 1.1 because in

HTML all whitespace, including carriage returns and multiple space or tab characters, is displayed as a single space in a rendered web page.

A newline character inside a PHP code block does not form part of the output. Line breaks can be used to format the code in a readable way, but several short commands could appear on the same line of code, or a long command could span several lines—that's why you use the semicolon to indicate the end of a command.

Listing 1.3 is identical to Listing 1.2 except that the formatting makes this script almost unreadable.

LISTING 1.3   A Badly Formatted Script That Displays the Date and Time

```
<?php echo "The time is ";   echo date('H:i:s'); echo
" and the date is "
; echo date(
'j F Y'
);
?>
```

> **Using Newlines**   If you wanted to send an explicit newline character to the web browser, you could use the character sequence \n. There are several character sequences like this that have special meanings, and you will see more of them in Lesson 6, "Working with Strings."

Comments

Another way to make sure your code remains readable is by adding comments to it. A *comment* is a piece of free text that can appear anywhere in a script and is completely ignored by PHP. The different comment styles supported by PHP are shown in Table 1.1.

TABLE 1.1   Comment Styles in PHP

Comment	Description
// or #	Single-line comment. Everything to the end of the current line is ignored.
/* ... */	Single- or multiple-line comment. Everything between /* and */ is ignored.

Listing 1.4 produces the same formatted date and time as Listings 1.1, 1.2, and 1.3, but it contains an abundance of comments. Because the comments are just ignored by PHP, the output produced consists of only the date and time.

LISTING 1.4   Using Comments in a Script

```php
<?php
/* time.php
   This script prints the current date
   and time in the web browser
*/

echo "The time is ";
echo date('H:i:s');  // Hours, minutes, seconds

echo " and the date is ";
echo date('j F Y');  // Day name, month name, year
?>
```

Listing 1.4 includes a header comment block that contains the filename and a brief description, as well as inline comments that show what each date command will produce.

Summary

In this lesson you have learned how PHP works in a web environment, and you have seen what a simple PHP script looks like. In the next lesson you will learn how to use variables.

Lesson 2
Variables

In this lesson you will learn how to assign values to variables in PHP and use them in some simple expressions.

Understanding Variables

Variables—containers in which values can be stored and later retrieved— are a fundamental building block of any programming language.

For instance, you could have a variable called number that holds the value 5 or a variable called name that holds the value Chris. The following PHP code declares variables with those names and values:

```
$number = 5;
$name = "Chris";
```

In PHP, a variable name is always prefixed with a dollar sign. If you remember that, declaring a new variable is very easy: You just use an equals symbol with the variable name on the left and the value you want it to take on the right.

> **Declaring Variables**   Unlike in some programming languages, in PHP variables do not need to be declared before they can be used. You can assign a value to a new variable name any time you want to start using it.

Variables can be used in place of fixed values throughout the PHP language. The following example uses echo to display the value stored in a variable in the same way that you would display a piece of fixed text:

```
$name = "Chris";
echo "Hello, ";
echo $name;
```

The output produced is

```
Hello, Chris
```

Naming Variables

The more descriptive your variable names are, the more easily you will remember what they are used for when you come back to a script several months after you write it.

It is not usually a good idea to call your variables $a, $b, and so on. You probably won't remember what each letter stood for, if anything, for long. Good variable names tell exactly what kind of value you can expect to find stored in them (for example, $price or $name).

Case-Sensitivity   Variable names in PHP are case-sensitive. For example, $name is a different variable than $Name, and the two could store different values in the same script.

Variable names can contain only letters, numbers, and the underscore character, and each must begin with a letter or underscore. Table 2.1 shows some examples of valid and invalid variable names.

TABLE 2.1   Examples of Valid and Invalid Variable Names

Valid Variable Names	Invalid Variable Names
$percent	$pct%
$first_name	$first-name
$line_2	$2nd_line

> **Using Underscores**   Using the underscore character is
> a handy way to give a variable a name that is made
> up of two or more words. For example $first_name
> and $date_of_birth are more readable for having
> underscores in place.
>
> Another popular convention for combining words is
> to capitalize the first letter of each word—for exam-
> ple, $FirstName and $DateOfBirth. If you prefer this
> style, feel free to use it in your scripts but remember
> that the capitalization does matter.

Expressions

When a variable assignment takes place, the value given does not have to
be a fixed value. It could be an *expression*—two or more values combined
using an *operator* to produce a result. It should be fairly obvious how the
following example works, but the following text breaks it down into its
components:

```
$sum = 16 + 30;
echo $sum;
```

The variable $sum takes the value of the expression to the right of the
equals sign. The values 16 and 30 are combined using the addition operator—the plus symbol (+)—and the result of adding the two values
together is returned. As expected, this piece of code displays the value 46.

To show that variables can be used in place of fixed values, you can perform the same addition operation on two variables:

```
$a = 16;
$b = 30;
$sum = $a + $b;
echo $sum;
```

The values of $a and $b are added together, and once again, the output
produced is 46.

Variables in Strings

You have already seen that text strings need to be enclosed in quotation marks and learned that there is a difference between single and double quotes.

The difference is that a dollar sign in a double-quoted string indicates that the current value of that variable should become part of the string. In a single-quoted string, on the other hand, the dollar sign is treated as a literal character, and no reference is made to any variables.

The following examples should help explain this. In the following example, the value of variable $name is included in the string:

```
$name = "Chris";
echo "Hello, $name";
```

This code displays Hello, Chris.

In the following example, this time the dollar sign is treated as a literal, and no variable substitution takes place:

```
$name = 'Chris';
echo 'Hello, $name';
```

This code displays Hello, $name.

Sometimes you need to indicate to PHP exactly where a variable starts and ends. You do this by using curly brackets, or *braces* ({}). If you wanted to display a weight value with a suffix to indicate pounds or ounces, the statement might look like this:

```
echo "The total weight is {$weight}lb";
```

If you did not use the braces around $weight, PHP would try to find the value of $weightlb, which probably does not exist in your script.

You could do the same thing by using the *concatenation* operator, the period symbol, which can be used to join two or more strings together, as shown in the following example:

```
echo 'The total weight is ' . $weight . 'lb';
```

The three values—two fixed strings and the variable $weight—are simply stuck together in the order in which they appear in the statement. Notice that a space is included at the end of the first string because you want the value of $weight to be joined to the word is.

If $weight has a value of 99, this statement will produce the following output:

```
The total weight is 99lb
```

Data Types

Every variable that holds a value also has a data type that defines what kind of value it is holding. The basic data types in PHP are shown in Table 2.2.

TABLE 2.2 PHP Data Types

Data Type	Description
Boolean	A truth value; can be either TRUE or FALSE.
Integer	A number value; can be a positive or negative whole number.
Double (or float)	A floating-point number value; can be any decimal number.
String	An alphanumeric value; can contain any number of ASCII characters.

When you assign a value to a variable, the data type of the variable is also set. PHP determines the data type automatically, based on the value you assign. If you want to check what data type PHP thinks a value is, you can use the gettype function.

Running the following code shows that the data type of a decimal number is double:

```
$value = 7.2;
echo gettype($value);
```

The complementary function to `gettype` is `settype`, which allows you to override the data type of a variable. If the stored value is not suitable to be stored in the new type, it will be modified to the closest value possible.

The following code attempts to convert a string value into an integer:

```
$value =  "22nd January 2005";
settype($value, "integer");
echo $value;
```

In this case, the string begins with numbers, but the whole string is not an integer. The conversion converts everything up to the first nonnumeric character and discards the rest, so the output produced is just the number 22.

> **Analyzing Data Types** In practice, you will not use `settype` and `gettype` very often because you will rarely need to alter the data type of a variable. This book covers this topic early on so that you are aware that PHP does assign a data type to every variable.

Type Juggling

Sometimes PHP will perform an implicit data type conversion if values are expected to be of a particular type. This is known as *type juggling*.

For example, the addition operator expects to sit between two numbers. String type values are converted to double or integer before the operation is performed, so the following addition produces an integer result:

```
echo 100 + "10 inches";
```

This expression adds 100 and 10, and it displays the result 110.

A similar thing happens when a string operator is used on numeric data. If you perform a string operation on a numeric type, the numeric value is converted to a string first. In fact, you already saw this earlier in this lesson, with the concatenation operator—the value of `$weight` that was displayed was numeric.

The result of a string operation will always be a string data type, even if it looks like a number. The following example produces the result 69, but—as gettype shows—$number contains a string value:

```
$number = 6 . 9;
echo $number;
echo gettype(6 . 9);
```

We will look at the powerful range of operators that are related to numeric and string data types in PHP in Lessons 5, "Working with Numbers," and 6, "Working with Strings."

Variable Variables

It is possible to use the value stored in a variable as the name of another variable. If this sounds confusing, the following example might help:

```
$my_age = 21;
$varname = "my_age";
echo "The value of $varname is ${$varname}";
```

The output produced is

```
The value of my_age is 21
```

Because this string is enclosed in double quotes, a dollar sign indicates that a variable's value should become part of the string. The construct ${$varname} indicates that the value of the variable named in $varname should become part of the string and is known as a *variable variable*.

The braces around $varname are used to indicate that it should be referenced first; they are required in double-quoted strings but are otherwise optional. The following example produces the same output as the preceding example, using the concatenation operator:

```
echo 'The value of ' . $varname . ' is ' . $$varname;
```

Summary

In this lesson you have learned how variables work in PHP. In the next lesson you will see how to use conditional and looping statements to control the flow of your script.

LESSON 3
Flow Control

In this lesson you will learn about the conditional and looping constructs that allow you to control the flow of a PHP script.

In this chapter we'll look at two types of flow control: conditional statements, which tell your script to execute a section of code only if certain criteria are met, and loops, which indicate a block of code that is to be repeated a number of times.

Conditional Statements

A conditional statement in PHP begins with the keyword `if`, followed by a condition in parentheses. The following example checks whether the value of the variable `$number` is less than 10, and the `echo` statement displays its message only if this is the case:

```
$number = 5;
if ($number < 10) {
    echo "$number is less than ten";
}
```

The condition `$number < 10` is satisfied if the value on the left of the `<` symbol is smaller than the value on the right. If this condition holds true, then the code in the following set of braces will be executed; otherwise, the script jumps to the next statement after the closing brace.

> **Boolean Values**   Every conditional expression evaluates to a Boolean value, and an `if` statement simply acts on a TRUE or FALSE value to determine whether the next block of code should be executed. Any zero value in PHP is considered FALSE, and any nonzero value is considered TRUE.

As it stands, the previous example will be TRUE because 5 is less than 10, so the statement in braces is executed, and the corresponding output is displayed. Now, if you change the initial value of $number to 10 or higher and rerun the script, the condition fails, and no output is produced.

Braces are used in PHP to group blocks of code together. In a conditional statement, they surround the section of code that is to be executed if the preceding condition is true.

Brackets and Braces   You will come across three types of brackets when writing PHP scripts. The most commonly used terminology for each type is parentheses (( )), braces ({ }), and square brackets ([ ]).

Braces are not required after an if statement. If they are omitted, the following single statement is executed if the condition is true. Any subsequent statements are executed, regardless of the status of the conditional.

Braces and Indentation   Although how your code is indented makes no difference to PHP, it is customary to indent blocks of code inside braces with a few space characters to visually separate that block from other statements.

Even if you only want a condition or loop to apply to one statement, it is still useful to use braces for clarity. It is particularly important in order to keep things readable when you're nesting multiple constructs.

Conditional Operators

PHP allows you to perform a number of different comparisons, to check for the equality or relative size of two values. PHP's conditional operators are shown in Table 3.1.

TABLE 3.1   Conditional Operators in PHP

Operator	Description
==	Is equal to
===	Is identical to (is equal and is the same data type)
!=	Is not equal to
!==	Is not identical to
<	Is less than
<=	Is less than or equal to
>	Is greater than
>=	Is greater than or equal to

= or ==?   Be careful when comparing for equality to use a double equals symbol (==). A single = is always an assignment operator and, unless the value assigned is zero, your condition will always return true—and remember that TRUE is any nonzero value. Always use == when comparing two values to avoid headaches.

Logical Operators

You can combine multiple expressions to check two or more criteria in a single conditional statement. For example, the following statement checks whether the value of $number is between 5 and 10:

```
$number = 8;
if ($number >= 5 and $number <= 10) {
   echo "$number is between five and ten";
}
```

The keyword and is a *logical operator*, which signifies that the overall condition will be true only if the expressions on either side are true. That is, $number has to be both greater than or equal to 5 and less than or equal to 10.

Table 3.2 shows the logical operators that can be used in PHP.

TABLE 3.2   Logical Operators in PHP

Operator	Name	Description
! a	NOT	True if a is not true
a && b	AND	True if both a and b are true
a || b	OR	True if either a or b is true
a and b	AND	True if both a and b are true
a xor b	XOR	True if a or b is true, but not both
a or b	OR	True if either a or b is true

You may have noticed that there are two different ways of performing a logical AND or OR in PHP. The difference between and and && (and between or and ||) is the precedence used to evaluate expressions.

Table 3.2 lists the highest-precedence operators first. The following conditions, which appear to do the same thing, are subtly but significantly different:

a or b and c
a || b and c

In the former condition, the and takes precedence and is evaluated first. The overall condition is true if a is true or if both b and c are true.

In the latter condition, the || takes precedence, so c must be true, as must either a or b, to satisfy the condition.

Operator Symbols   Note that the logical AND and OR operators are the double symbols && and ||, respectively. These symbols, when used singularly, have a different meaning, as you will see in Lesson 5, "Working with Numbers."

Multiple Condition Branches

By using an `else` clause with an `if` statement, you can specify an alternate action to be taken if the condition is not met. The following example tests the value of `$number` and displays a message that says whether it is greater than or less than 10:

```
$number = 16;
if ($number < 10) {
  echo "$number is less than ten";
}
else {
  echo "$number is more than ten";
}
```

The `else` clause provides an either/or mechanism for conditional statements. To add more branches to a conditional statement, the `elseif` keyword can be used to add a further condition that is checked only if the previous condition in the statement fails.

The following example uses the `date` function to find the current time of day—`date("H")` gives a number between 0 and 23 that represents the hour on the clock—and displays an appropriate greeting:

```
$hour = date("H");
if ($hour < 12) {
  echo "Good morning";
}
elseif ($hour < 17) {
  echo "Good afternoon";
}
else {
  echo "Good evening";
}
```

This code displays Good morning if the server time is between midnight and 11:59, Good afternoon from midday to 4:59 p.m., and Good evening from 5 p.m. onward.

Notice that the `elseif` condition only checks that `$hour` is less than 17 (5 p.m.). It does not need to check that the value is between 12 and 17 because the initial `if` condition ensures that PHP will not get as far as the `elseif` if `$hour` is less than 12.

The code in the else clause is executed if all else fails. For values of $hour that are 17 or higher, neither the if nor the elseif condition will be true.

> ✎ **elseif Versus else if** In PHP you can also write elseif as two words: else if. The way PHP interprets this variation is slightly different, but its behavior is exactly the same.

The switch Statement

An if statement can contain as many elseif clauses as you need, but including many of these clauses can often create cumbersome code, and an alternative is available. switch is a conditional statement that can have multiple branches in a much more compact format.

The following example uses a switch statement to check $name against two lists to see whether it belongs to a friend:

```
switch ($name) {
  case "Damon":
  case "Shelley":
    echo "Welcome, $name, you are my friend";
    break;
  case "Adolf":
  case "Saddam":
    echo "You are no friend of mine, $name";
    break;
  default:
    echo "I do not know who you are, $name";
}
```

Each case statement defines a value for which the next block of PHP code will be executed. If you assign your first name to $name and run this script, you will be greeted as a friend if your name is Damon or Shelley, and you will be told that you are not a friend if your name is either Adolf or Saddam. If you have any other name, the script will tell you it does not know who you are.

There can be any number of `case` statements preceding the PHP code to which they relate. If the value that is being tested by the `switch` statement (in this case `$name`) matches any one of them, any subsequent PHP code will be executed until a `break` command is reached.

Breaking Out The `break` statement is important in a `switch` statement. When a `case` statement has been matched, any PHP code that follows will be executed—even if there is another `case` statement checking for a different value. This behavior can sometimes be useful, but mostly it is not what you want—so remember to put a `break` after every `case`.

Any other value for `$name` will cause the `default` code block to be executed. As with an `else` clause, `default` is optional and supplies an action to be taken if nothing else is appropriate.

Loops

PHP offers three types of loop constructs that all do the same thing—repeat a section of code a number of times—in slightly different ways.

The `while` Loop

The `while` keyword takes a condition in parentheses, and the code block that follows is repeated while that condition is true. If the condition is false initially, the code block will not be repeated at all.

Infinite Loops The repeating code must perform some action that affects the condition in such a way that the loop condition will eventually no longer be met; otherwise, the loop will repeat forever.

The following example uses a `while` loop to display the square numbers from 1 to 10:

```
$count = 1;
while ($count <= 10) {
   $square = $count * $count;
   echo "$count squared is $square <br>";
   $count++;
}
```

The counter variable `$count` is initialized with a value of 1. The `while` loop calculates the square of that number and displays it, then adds one to the value of `$count`. The `++` operator adds one to the value of the variable that precedes it.

The loop repeats while the condition `$count <= 10` is true, so the first 10 numbers and their squares are displayed in turn, and then the loop ends.

The do Loop

The do loop is very similar to the `while` loop except that the condition comes after the block of repeating code. Because of this variation, the loop code is always executed at least once—even if the condition is initially false.

The following do loop is equivalent to the previous example, displaying the numbers from 1 to 10, with their squares:

```
$count = 1;
do {
   $square = $count * $count;
   echo "$count squared is $square <br>";
   $count++;
} while ($count <= 10);
```

The for Loop

The `for` loop provides a compact way to create a loop. The following example performs the same loop as the previous two examples:

```
for ($count = 1; $count <= 10; $count++) {
   $square = $count * $count;
   echo "$count squared is $square <br>";
}
```

As you can see, using `for` allows you to use much less code to do the same thing as with `while` and `do`.

A `for` statement has three parts, separated by semicolons:

- The first part is an expression that is evaluated once when the loop begins. In the preceding example, you initialized the value of `$count`.

- The second part is the condition. While the condition is true, the loop continues repeating. As with a `while` loop, if the condition is false to start with, the following code block is not executed at all.

- The third part is an expression that is evaluated once at the end of each pass of the loop. In the previous example, `$count` is incremented after each line of the output is displayed.

Nesting Conditions and Loops

So far you have only seen simple examples of conditions and loops. However, you can nest these constructs within each other to create some quite complex rules to control the flow of a script.

> **Remember to Indent**   The more complex the flow control in your script is, the more important it becomes to indent your code to make it clear which blocks of code correspond to which constructs.

Breaking Out of a Loop

You have already learned about using the keyword `break` in a `switch` statement. You can also use `break` in a loop construct to tell PHP to immediately exit the loop and continue with the rest of the script.

The `continue` keyword is used to end the current pass of a loop. However, unlike with `break`, the script jumps back to the top of the same loop and continues execution until the loop condition fails.

Summary

In this lesson you have learned how to vary the flow of your PHP script by using conditional statements and loops. In the next lesson you will see how to create reusable functions from blocks of PHP code.

LESSON 4
Functions

In this lesson you will learn how frequently used sections of code can be turned into reusable functions.

Using Functions

A *function* is used to make a task that might consist of many lines of code into a routine that can be called using a single instruction.

PHP contains many functions that perform a wide range of useful tasks. Some are built in to the PHP language; others are more specialized and are available only if certain extensions are activated when PHP is installed.

The online PHP manual (www.php.net) is an invaluable reference. As well as documentation for every function in the language, the manual pages are also annotated with user-submitted tips and examples, and you can even submit your own comments if you want.

> **Online Reference**   To quickly pull up the PHP manual page for any function, use this shortcut: www.php.net/*function_name*.

You have already used the date function to generate a string that contains a formatted version of the current date. Let's take a closer look at how that example from Lesson 1, "Getting to Know PHP," works. The example looked like this:

```
echo date('j F Y');
```

The online PHP manual gives the prototype for date as follows:

```
string date (string format [, int timestamp])
```

This means that date takes a string argument called format and, optionally, the integer timestamp. It returns a string value. This example sends j
F Y to the function as the format argument, but timestamp is omitted. The
echo command displays the string that is returned.

> **Prototypes**   Every function has a prototype that
> defines how many arguments it takes, the arguments'
> data types, and what value is returned. Optional argu-
> ments are shown in square brackets ([ ]).

Defining Functions

In addition to the built-in functions, PHP allows you to define your own.
There are advantages to using your own function. Not only do you have to
type less when the same piece of code has to be executed several times
but a custom-defined function also makes your script easier to maintain. If
you want to change the way a task is performed, you only need to update
the program code once—in the function definition—rather than fix it
every place it appears in your script.

> **Modular Code**   Grouping tasks into functions is the
> first step toward *modularizing* your code—something
> that is especially important to keep your scripts man-
> ageable as they grow in size and become more com-
> plex.

The following is a simple example that shows how a function is defined
and used in PHP:

```php
function add_tax($amount) {
  $total = $amount * 1.09;
  return $total;
}

$price = 16.00;
echo "Price before tax: $price <br>";
```

```
echo "Price after tax: ";
echo add_tax($price);
```

The function keyword defines a function called add_tax that will execute the code block that follows. The code that makes up a function is always contained in braces. Putting $amount in parentheses after the function name stipulates that add_tax takes a single argument that will be stored in a variable called $amount inside the function.

The first line of the function code is a simple calculation that multiplies $amount by 1.09—which is equivalent to adding 9% to that value—and assigns the result to $total. The return keyword is followed by the value that is to be returned when the function is called from within the script.

Running this example produces the following output:

```
Price before tax: 16
Price after tax: 17.44
```

This is an example of a function that you might use in many places in a web page; for instance, on a page that lists all the products available in an online store, you would call this function once for each item that is displayed to show the after-tax price. If the rate of tax changes, you only need to change the formula in add_tax to alter every price displayed on that page.

Arguments and Return Values

Every function call consists of the function name followed by a list of arguments in parentheses. If there is more than one argument, the list items are separated with commas. Some functions do not require any arguments at all, but a pair of parentheses is still required—even if there are no arguments contained in them.

The built-in function phpinfo generates a web page that contains a lot of information about the PHP module. This function does not require any arguments, so it can be called from a script that is as simple as

```
<?php phpinfo();?>
```

If you create this script and point a web browser at it, you will see a web page that contains system information and configuration settings.

Returning Success or Failure

Because phpinfo generates its own output, you do not need to prefix it with echo, but, for the same reason, you cannot assign the web page it produces to a variable. In fact, the return value from phpinfo is the integer value 1.

> **Returning True and False**   Functions that do not have an explicit return value usually use a return code to indicate whether their operation has completed successfully. A zero value (FALSE) indicates failure, and a nonzero value (TRUE) indicates success.

The following example uses the mail function to attempt to send an email from a PHP script. The first three arguments to mail specify the recipient's email address, the message subject, and the message body. The return value of mail is used in an if condition to check whether the function was successful:

```
if (mail("chris@lightwood.net",
         "Hello", "This is a test email")) {
  echo "Email was sent successfully";
}
else {
  echo "Email could not be sent";
}
```

If the web server that this script is run on is not properly configured to send email, or if there is some other error when trying to send, mail will return zero, indicating that the email could not be sent. A nonzero value indicates that the message was handed off to your mail server for sending.

> **Return Values**   Although you will not always need to
> test the return value of every function, you should be
> aware that every function in PHP does return some
> value.

Default Argument Values

The mail function is an example of a function that takes multiple arguments; the recipient, subject, and message body are all required. The prototype for mail also specifies that this function can take an optional fourth argument, which can contain additional mail headers.

Calling mail with too few arguments results in a warning. For instance, a script that contains the following:

```
mail("chris@lightwood.net", "Hello");
```

will produce a warning similar to this:

```
Warning: mail() expects at least 3 parameters, 2 given in
/home/chris/mail.php on line 3
```

However, the following two calls to mail are both valid:

```
mail("chris@lightwood.net", "Hello", "This is a test email");

mail("chris@lightwood.net", "Hello", "This is a test email",
    "Cc: editor@samspublishing.com");
```

To have more than one argument in your own function, you simply use a comma-separated list of variable names in the function definition. To make one of these arguments optional, you assign it a default value in the argument list, the same way you would assign a value to a variable.

The following example is a variation of add_tax that takes two arguments—the net amount and the tax rate to add on. $rate has a default value of 10, so it is an optional argument:

```
function add_tax_rate($amount, $rate=10) {
  $total = $amount * (1 + ($rate / 100));
  return($total);
}
```

Using this function, the following two calls are both valid:

```
add_tax_rate(16);
add_tax_rate(16, 9);
```

The first example uses the default rate of 10%, whereas the second example specifies a rate of 9% to be used—producing the same behavior as the original add_tax function example.

Optional Arguments   All the optional arguments to a function must appear at the end of the argument list, with the required values passed in first. Otherwise, PHP will not know which arguments you are passing to the function.

Variable Scope

The reason values have to be passed in to functions as arguments has to do with *variable scope*—the rules that determine what sections of script are able to access which variables.

The basic rule is that any variables defined in the main body of the script cannot be used inside a function. Likewise, any variables used inside a function cannot be seen by the main script.

Scope   Variables available within a function are said to be *local variables* or that their scope is local to that function. Variables that are not local are called *global variables*.

Local and global variables can have the same name and contain different values, although it is best to try to avoid this to make your script easier to read.

When called, add_tax calculates $total, and this is the value returned. However, even after add_tax is called, the local variable $total is undefined outside that function.

The following piece of code attempts to display the value of a global variable from inside a function:

```
function display_value() {
   echo $value;
}

$value = 125;
display_value();
```

If you run this script, you will see that no output is produced because $value has not been declared in the local scope.

To access a global variable inside a function, you must use the global keyword at the top of the function code. Doing so overrides the scope of that variable so that it can be read and altered within the function. The following code shows an example:

```
function change_value() {
   global $value;
   echo "Before: $value <br>";
   $value = $value * 2;
}
$value = 100;
display_value();
echo "After: $value <br>";
```

The value of $value can now be accessed inside the function, so the output produced is as follows:

```
Before: 100
After: 200
```

Using Library Files

After you have created a function that does something useful, you will probably want to use it again in other scripts. Rather than copy the function definition into each script that needs to use it, you can use a library file so that your function needs to be stored and maintained in only one place.

Before you go any further, you should create a library file called tax.php that contains both the add_tax and add_tax_rate functions but no other PHP code.

Using Library Files A library file needs to enclose its PHP code inside <?php tags just like a regular script; otherwise, the contents will be displayed as HTML when they are included in a script.

Including Library Files

To incorporate an external library file into another script, you use the include keyword. The following includes tax.php so that add_tax can be called in that script:

```
include "tax.php";
$price = 95;
echo "Price before tax: $price <br>";
echo "Price after tax: ";
echo add_tax($price);
```

The include path Setting By default, include searches only the current directory and a few system locations for files to be included. If you want to include files from another location, you can use a path to the file.

You can extend the include path to include other locations without a path being required by changing the value of the include_path setting. Refer to Lesson 23, "PHP," for more information.

You can use the include_once keyword if you want to make sure that a library file is loaded only once. If a script attempts to define the same function a second time, an error will result. Using include_once helps to avoid this, particularly when files are being included from other library files. It is often useful to have a library file that includes several other files, each containing a few functions, rather than one huge library file.

> **Require** The require and require_once instructions
> work in a similar way to include and include_once but
> have subtly different behavior. In the event of an
> error, include generates a warning, but the script car-
> ries on running as best it can. A failure from a require
> statement causes the script to exit immediately.

Summary

In this lesson you have learned how to use functions to modularize your
code. In the next lesson you will learn about ways to work with numeric
data in PHP.

Lesson 5
Working with Numbers

In this lesson you will learn about some of the numeric manipulations you can perform in PHP.

Arithmetic

As you would expect, PHP includes all the basic arithmetic operators. If you have not used another programming language, the symbols used might not all be obvious, so we'll quickly run through the basic rules of arithmetic in PHP.

Arithmetic Operators

Addition is performed with the plus symbol (+). This example adds 6 and 12 together and displays the result:

```
echo 6 + 12;
```

Subtraction is performed with the minus symbol (-), which is also used as a hyphen. This example subtracts 5 from 24:

```
echo 24 - 5;
```

The minus symbol can also be used to negate a number (for example, -20).

Multiplication is performed with the asterisk symbol (*). This example displays the product of 4 and 9:

```
echo 4 * 9;
```

Division is performed with the forward slash symbol (/). This example divides 48 by 12:

```
echo 48 / 12;
```

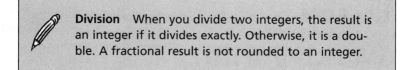

> **Division**   When you divide two integers, the result is an integer if it divides exactly. Otherwise, it is a double. A fractional result is not rounded to an integer.

Modulus is performed by using the percent symbol (%). This example displays 3—the remainder of 21 divided by 6:

```
echo 21 % 6;
```

> **Modulus**   The modulus operator can be used to test whether a number is odd or even by using $number % 2. The result will be 0 for all even numbers and 1 for all odd numbers (because any odd number divided by 2 has a remainder of 1).

Incrementing and Decrementing

In PHP you can increment or decrement a number by using a double plus (++) or double minus (- -) symbol. The following statements both add one to $number:

```
$number++;
```

```
++$number;
```

The operator can be placed on either side of a variable, and its position determines at what point the increment takes place.

This statement subtracts one from $countdown before displaying the result:

```
echo --$countdown;
```

However, the following statement displays the current value of $countdown before decrementing it:

```
echo $countdown--;
```

The increment and decrement operators are commonly used in loops. The following is a typical for loop, using a counter to repeat a section of code 10 times:

```
for ($count=1; $count<=10; $count++) {
  echo "Count = $count<br>";
}
```

In this case, the code simply outputs the value of $count for each pass of the loop.

Compound Operators

Compound operators provide a handy shortcut when you want to apply an arithmetic operation to an existing variable. The following example uses the compound addition operator to add six to the current value of $count:

```
$count += 6;
```

The effect of this is to take the initial value of $count, add six to it, and then assign it back to $count. In fact, the operation is equivalent to doing the following:

```
$count = $count + 6;
```

All the basic arithmetic operators have corresponding compound operators, as shown in Table 5.1.

TABLE 5.1   Compound Operators

Operator	Equivalent To
$a += $b	$a = $a + $b;
$a -= $b	$a = $a - $b;
$a *= $b	$a = $a * $b;
$a /= $b	$a = $a / $b;
$a %= $b	$a = $a % $b;

Operator Precedence

The rules governing operator precedence specify the order in which expressions are evaluated. For example, the following statement is ambiguous:

```
echo 3 * 4 + 5;
```

Are 3 and 4 multiplied together, and then 5 is added to the result, giving a total of 17? Or are 4 and 5 added together first and multiplied by 3, giving 27? Running this statement in a script will show you that in PHP, the result is 17.

The reason is that multiplication has a higher precedence than addition, so when these operators appear in the same expression, multiplication takes place first, using the values that immediately surround the multiplication operator.

To tell PHP that you explicitly want the addition to take place first, you can use parentheses, as in the following example:

```
echo 3 * (4 + 5);
```

In this case, the result is 27.

In PHP, the precedence of arithmetic operators follows the PEMDAS rule that you may have learned at school: parentheses, exponentiation, multiplication/division, and addition/subtraction.

The full operator precedence list for PHP, including many operators you haven't come across yet, can be found in the online manual at www.php.net/manual/en/language.operators.php.

Numeric Data Types

You have already seen that PHP assigns a data type to each value and that the numeric data types are integer and double, for whole numbers.

To check whether a value is either of these types, you use the is_float and is_int functions. Likewise, to check for either numeric data type in one operation, you can use is_numeric.

The following example contains a condition that checks whether the value of $number is an integer:

```php
$number = "28";
if (is_int($number)) {
  echo "$number is an integer";
}
else {
  echo "$number is not an integer";
}
```

Because the actual declaration of that variable assigns a string value—albeit one that contains a number—the condition fails.

Although $number in the previous example is a string, PHP is flexible enough to allow this value to be used in numeric operations. The following example shows that a string value that contains a number can be incremented and that the resulting value is an integer:

```php
$number = "6";
$number++;
echo "$number has type " . gettype($number);
```

Understanding NULLs

The value NULL is a data type all to itself—a value that actually has no value. It has no numeric value, but comparing to an integer value zero evaluates to true:

```php
$number = 0;
$empty=NULL;
if ($number == $empty) {
  echo "The values are the same";
}
```

> **Type Comparisons** If you want to check that both the values and data types are the same in a condition, you use the triple equals comparison operator (===).

Numeric Functions

Let's take a look at some of the numeric functions available in PHP.

Rounding Numbers

There are three different PHP functions for rounding a decimal number to an integer.

You use `ceil` or `floor` to round a number up or down to the nearest integer, respectively. For example, `ceil(1.3)` returns 2, whereas `floor(6.8)` returns 6.

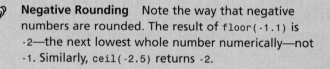

Negative Rounding   Note the way that negative numbers are rounded. The result of `floor(-1.1)` is -2—the next lowest whole number numerically—not -1. Similarly, `ceil(-2.5)` returns -2.

To round a value to the nearest whole number, you use `round`. A fractional part under .5 will be rounded down, whereas .5 or higher will be rounded up. For example, `round(1.3)` returns 1, whereas `round(1.5)` returns 2.

The `round` function can also take an optional precision argument. The following example displays a value rounded to two decimal places:

```
$score = 0.535;
echo round($score, 2);
```

The value displayed is `0.54`; the third decimal place being 5 causes the final digit to be rounded up.

You can also use `round` with a negative precision value to round an integer to a number of significant figures, as in the following example:

```
$distance = 2834;
echo round($distance, -2);
```

Comparisons

To find the smallest and largest of a group of numbers, you use min and max, respectively. These functions take two or more arguments and return the numerically lowest or highest element in the list, respectively.

This statement will display the larger of the two variables $a and $b:

```
echo max($a, $b);
```

There is no limit to the number of arguments that can be compared. The following example finds the lowest value from a larger set of values:

```
echo min(6, 10, 23, 3, 88, 102, 5, 44);
```

Not surprisingly, the result displayed is 3.

Random Numbers

You use rand to generate a random integer, using your system's built-in random number generator. The rand function optionally takes two arguments that specify the range of numbers from which the random number will be picked.

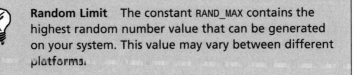

Random Limit   The constant RAND_MAX contains the highest random number value that can be generated on your system. This value may vary between different platforms.

The following statement picks a random number between 1 and 10 and displays it:

```
echo rand(1, 10);
```

You can put this command in a script and run it a few times to see that the number changes each time it is run.

There is really no such thing as a computer-generated random number. In fact, numbers are actually picked from a very long sequence that has very similar properties to true random numbers. To make sure you always start from a different place in this sequence, you have to *seed* the random number generator by calling the srand function; no arguments are required.

> **Random Algorithms**   PHP includes another random number generator, known as Mersenne Twister, that is considered to produce better random results than rand. To use this algorithm, you use the functions mt_rand and mt_srand.

Mathematical Functions

PHP includes many mathematical functions, including trigonometry, logarithms, and number base conversions. As you will rarely need to use these in a web environment, those functions are not covered in this book.

To find out about a function that performs a specific mathematical purpose, refer to the online manual at www.php.net/manual/en/ref.math.php.

Summary

In this lesson you have learned how to work with numbers. In the next lesson you will learn all about string handling in PHP.

LESSON 6
Working with Strings

In this lesson you will learn about some of the powerful string functions that are included in the PHP language.

Anatomy of a String

A *string* is a collection of characters that is treated as a single entity. In PHP, strings are enclosed in quotation marks, and you can declare a string type variable by assigning it a string that is contained in either single or double quotes.

The following examples are identical; both create a variable called $phrase that contains the phrase shown:

```
$phrase = "The sky is falling";
$phrase = 'The sky is falling';
```

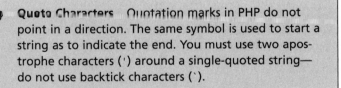

Quote Characters Quotation marks in PHP do not point in a direction. The same symbol is used to start a string as to indicate the end. You must use two apostrophe characters (') around a single-quoted string—do not use backtick characters (`).

Escaping Characters with Backslash

Double quotes can be used within single-quoted strings and vice versa. For instance, these string assignments are both valid:

```
$phrase = "It's time to party!";
$phrase = 'So I said, "OK"';
```

However, if you want to use the same character within a quoted string, you must escape that quote by using a backslash. The following examples demonstrate this:

```
$phrase = 'It\'s time to party!";
$phrase = "So I said, \"OK\"";
```

In the previous examples, if the backslash were not used, PHP would mismatch the quotes, and an error would result.

Which style of quoting you use largely depends on personal preference and, hopefully, a desire to create tidy code. Remember, though, as you saw in Lesson 2, "Variables," that a variable prefixed with a dollar sign inside a double-quoted string is replaced with its values, whereas in a single-quoted string, the dollar sign and variable name appear verbatim.

If you want a dollar sign to form part of a double-quoted string, you can also escape this by using a backslash. For example, the following two statements are equivalent:

```
$offer = 'Save $10 on first purchase';
$offer = "Save \$10 on first purchase";
```

Without the backslash, the second example would attempt to find the value of a variable called $10, which is, in fact, an illegal variable name.

The backslash character can also be used in a double-quoted string to indicate some special values inside strings. When followed by a three-digit number, it indicates the ASCII character with that octal value.

You can send the common nonprintable ASCII characters by using standard escape characters. A newline is \n, tab is \t, and so on. Refer to man ascii on your system or www.ascii.cl for a comprehensive list.

Concatenation

You have already seen how strings can be joined using the period symbol as a concatenation operator. A compound version of this operator, .=, can be used to append a string to an existing variable.

The following example builds up a string in stages and then displays the result:

```
$phrase = "I want ";
$phrase .= "to teach ";
$phrase .= "the world ";
$phrase .= "to sing";
echo $phrase;
```

The phrase appears as expected. Note the use of spaces after teach and
world to ensure that the final string is correctly spaced.

Comparing Strings

You can compare string values simply by using the standard comparison
operators. To check whether two strings are equal, you use the double
equals (==) sign:

```
if ($password == "letmein")
  echo "You have a guessable password";
```

The equality operator, when applied to strings, performs a case-sensitive
comparison. In the previous example, any other capitalization of
$password, such as LetMeIn, would not pass this test.

The inequality operators—<, <=, >, and >=—perform a comparison based
on the ASCII values of the individual characters in the strings. The following condition could be used to divide people into two groups, based
on their last name—those with names beginning A–M and those beginning N–Z:

```
if ($last_name < "N")
  echo "You are in group 1";
else
  echo "You are in group 2";
```

> **ASCII Values**   Because string comparisons are done on
> their underlying ASCII values, all lowercase letters
> have higher values than their equivalent uppercase
> letters. Letters a–z have values 97–122, whereas A–Z
> occupy values 65–90.

Formatting Strings

PHP provides a powerful way of creating formatted strings, using the
`printf` and `sprintf` functions. If you have used this function in C, these
will be quite familiar to you, although the syntax in PHP is a little
different.

Using `printf`

You use `printf` to display a formatted string. At its very simplest, `printf`
takes a single string argument and behaves the same as `echo`:

```
printf("Hello, world");
```

The power of `printf`, however, lies in its ability to substitute values into
placeholders in a string. Placeholders are identified by the percent character (%), followed by a format specification character.

The following example uses the simple format specifier %f to represent a
float number.

```
$price = 5.99;
printf("The price is %f", $price);
```

The second argument to `printf` is substituted in place of %f, so the following output is produced:

```
The price is 5.99
```

There is actually no limit to the number of substitution arguments in a
`printf` statement, as long as there are an equivalent number of placeholders in the string to be displayed. The following example demonstrates this
by adding in a string item:

```
$item = "The Origin of Species";
$price = 5.99;
printf("The price of %s is %f", $item, $price);
```

Table 6.1 shows the format characters that can be used with the `printf`
function in PHP to indicate different types of values.

TABLE 6.1 `printf` Format Characters

Character	Meaning
b	A binary (base 2) number
c	The ASCII character with the numeric value of the argument
d	A signed decimal (base 10) integer
e	A number displayed in scientific notation (for example, 2.6e+3)
u	An unsigned decimal integer
f	A floating-point number
o	An octal (base 8) number
s	A string
x	A hexadecimal (base 16) number with lowercase letters
X	A hexadecimal (base 16) number with uppercase letters

Suppose you use the %d format specifier instead of %f to display the value of $price:

```
$price = 5.99;
printf("As a decimal, the price is %d", $price);
```

In this case, PHP will treat the argument passed as an integer, so only the whole part of the value will be displayed. The output produced is as follows.

```
As a decimal, the price is 5
```

Decimals The %d format string represents a decimal integer, with *decimal* referring to base 10 numbers and not decimal points. There are different format specifiers to display numbers in base 16 (*hex*, %x), base 8 (*octal*, %o), and base 2 (*binary*, %b).

Format Codes

A format specifier can also include optional elements to specify the padding, alignment, width, and precision of the value to be displayed. This allows you to carry out some very powerful formatting.

The width specifier indicates how many characters the formatted value should occupy in the displayed string and appears between the percent sign and the type specifier. For instance, the following example ensures that the name displayed takes up exactly 10 characters:

```
$name1 = "Tom";
$name2 = "Dick";
$name3 = "Harry";
echo "<PRE>";
printf("%10s \n", $name1);
printf("%10s \n", $name2);
printf("%10s \n", $name3);
echo "</PRE>";
```

> **Padding** These examples use <PRE> tags to make sure that multiple spaces used for padding are displayed onscreen. Usually a web browser will treat multiple adjacent whitespace characters as a single space.
>
> String padding is not used very often in creating dynamic web pages. However, it is useful when you're producing plain-text output, such as generated email text, in PHP.

If you run this example through a web browser, you will see that each name displayed is indented from the left of the screen by the correct number of characters to make each name right-aligned with the others.

The default behavior is to right-align to the given width. However, you can reverse this by using the minus symbol as an alignment specifier. To left-align the strings in the previous example, you would use the format specifier %-10s. Although visibly this would not appear any different from simply using %s, the strings would be padded on the right with spaces to a length of 10 characters.

You can change the padding character from a space to any other character by placing that character before the width value, prefixed with a single quotation mark. The following example ensures that a five-digit order number is always displayed padded with zeros if necessary:

```
$order = 201;
printf("Order number: %'05d", $order);
```

The output produced is as follows:

```
Order number: 00201
```

The precision specifier is used with a floating-point number to specify the number of decimal places to display. The most common usage is with currency values, to ensure that the two cent digits always appear, even in a whole dollar amount.

The precision value follows the optional width specifier and is indicated by a period followed by the number of decimal places to display. The following example uses `%.2f` to display a currency value with no width specifier:

```
$price = 6;
printf("The price is %.2f", $price);
```

The price is correctly formatted as follows:

```
The price is 6.00
```

Float Widths   With floats, the width specifier indicates only the width of the number before the decimal point. For example, `%6.2f` will actually be nine characters long, with the period and two decimal places.

Using `sprintf`

The `sprintf` function is used to assign formatted strings to variables. The syntax is the same as for `printf`, but rather than being output as the result, the formatted value is returned by the function as a string.

For example, to assign a formatted price value to a new variable, you could do the following:

```
$new_price = sprintf("%.2f", $price);
```

All the format specifier rules that apply to `printf` also apply to `sprintf`.

String Functions

Let's take a look at some of the other string functions available in PHP. The full list of string functions can be found in the online manual, at www.php.net/manual/en/ref.strings.php.

Capitalization

You can switch the capitalization of a string to all uppercase or all lowercase by using `strtoupper` or `strtolower`, respectively.

The following example demonstrates the effect this has on a mixed-case string:

```
$phrase = "I love PHP";
echo strtoupper($phrase) . "<br>";
echo strtolower($phrase) . "<br>";
```

The result displayed is as follows:

```
I LOVE PHP
i love php
```

If you wanted to functions capitalize only the first character of a string, you use `ucfirst`:

```
$phrase = "welcome to the jungle";
echo $ucfirst($phrase);
```

You can also capitalize the first letter of each word—which is useful for names—by using `ucwords`:

```
$phrase = "green bay packers";
echo ucwords($phrase);
```

Neither ucfirst nor ucwords affects characters in the string that are
already in uppercase, so if you want to make sure that all the other characters are lowercase, you must combine these functions with strtolower,
as in the following example:

```
$name = "CHRIS NEWMAN";
echo ucwords(strtolower($name));
```

Dissecting a String

The substr function allows you to extract a substring by specifying a start
position within the string and a length argument. The following example
shows this in action:

```
$phrase = "I love PHP";
echo substr($phrase, 3, 5);
```

This call to substr returns the portion of $phrase from position 3 with a
length of 5 characters. Note that the position value begins at zero, not one,
so the actual substring displayed is ove P.

If the length argument is omitted, the value returned is the substring from
the position given to the end of the string. The following statement produces love PHP for $phrase:

```
echo substr($phrase, 2);
```

If the position argument is negative, substr counts from the end of the
string. For example, the following statement displays the last three characters of the string—in this case, PHP:

```
echo substr($phrase, -3);
```

If you need to know how long a string is, you use the strlen function:

```
echo strlen($phrase);
```

To find the position of a character or a string within another string, you
can use strpos. The first argument is often known as the *haystack*, and
the second as the *needle*, to indicate their relationship.

The following example displays the position of the @ character in an email address:

```
$email = "chris@lightwood.net";
echo strpos($email, "@");
```

String Positions   Remember that the character positions in a string are numbered from the left, starting from zero. Position 1 is actually the second character in the string. When `strpos` finds a match at the beginning of the string compared, the return value is zero, but when no match is found, the return value is FALSE.

You must check the type of the return value to determine this difference. For instance, the condition `strpos($a, $b)` === 0 holds true only when $b matches $a at the first character.

The `strstr` function extracts a portion of a string from the position at which a character or string appears up to the end of the string. This is a convenience function that saves your using a combination of `strpos` and `substr`.

The following two statements are equivalent:

```
$domain = strstr($email, "@");
```

```
$domain = strstr($email, strpos($email, "@"));
```

Summary

In this lesson you have learned how to work with strings in PHP. In the next lesson you will examine how regular expressions are used to perform pattern matching on strings.

LESSON 7

Working with Arrays

In this lesson you will learn how to use arrays in PHP to store and retrieve indexed data.

What Is an Array?

An *array* is a variable type that can store and index a set of values. An array is useful when the data you want to store has something in common or is logically grouped into a set.

Creating and Accessing Arrays

Suppose you wanted to store the average temperature for each month of the year. Using single-value variables—also known as *scalar variables*—you would need 12 different variables—$temp_jan, $temp_feb, and so on—to store the values. By using an array, you can use a single variable name to group the values together and let an index key indicate which month each value refers to.

The following PHP statement declares an array called $temps and assigns it 12 values that represent the temperatures for January through December:

```
$temps = array(38, 40, 49, 60, 70, 79,
               84, 83, 76, 65, 54, 42);
```

The array $temps that is created contains 12 values that are indexed with numeric key values from 0 to 11. To reference an indexed value from an array, you suffix the variable name with the index key. To display March's temperature, for example, you would use the following:

```
echo $temps[2];
```

Index Numbers   Because index values begin at zero by default, the value for March—the third month—is contained in the second element of the array.

The square brackets syntax can also be used to assign values to array elements. To set a new value for November, for instance, you could use the following:

```
$temps[10] = 56;
```

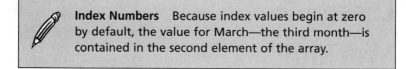 **The array Function**   The array function is a shortcut function that quickly builds an array from a supplied list of values, rather than adding each element in turn.

If you omit the index number when assigning an array element, the next highest index number will automatically be used. Starting with an empty array $temps, the following code would begin to build the same array as before:

```
$temps[] = 38;
$temps[] = 40;
$temps[] = 49;
...
```

In this example, the value 38 would be assigned to $temps[0], 40 to $temps[1], and so on. If you want to make sure that these assignments begin with $temps[0], it's a good idea to initialize the array first to make sure there is no existing data in that array. You can initialize the $temps array with the following command:

```
$temps = array();
```

Outputting the Contents of an Array

PHP includes a handy function, `print_r`, that can be used to recursively output all the values stored in an array. The following script defines the array of temperature values and then displays its contents onscreen:

```
$temps = array(38, 40, 49, 60, 70, 79,
                84, 83, 76, 65, 54, 42);
print "<PRE>";
print_r($temps);
print "</PRE>";
```

The <PRE> tags are needed around `print_r` because the output generated is text formatted with spaces and newlines. The output from this example is as follows:

```
Array
(
    [0] => 38
    [1] => 40
    [2] => 49
    [3] => 60
    [4] => 70
    [5] => 79
    [6] => 84
    [7] => 83
    [8] => 76
    [9] => 65
    [10] => 54
    [11] => 42
)
```

> **print_r** The `print_r` function can be very useful when you're developing scripts, although you will never use it as part of a live website. If you are ever unsure about what is going on in an array, using `print_r` can often shed light on the problem very quickly.

Looping Through an Array

You can easily replicate the way print_r loops through every element in an array by using a loop construct to perform another action for each value in the array.

By using a while loop, you can find all the index keys and their values from an array—similar to using the print_r function—as follows:

```
while (list($key, $value) = each($temps)) {
  echo "Key $key has value $val <br>";
}
```

For each element in the array, the index key value will be stored in $key and the value in $value.

PHP also provides another construct for traversing arrays in a loop, using a foreach construct. Whether you use a while or foreach loop is a matter of preference; you should use whichever you find easiest to read.

The foreach loop equivalent to the previous example is as follows:

```
foreach($temps as $key => $value) {
  . . .
}
```

Loops   You may have realized that with the $temps example, a for loop counting from 0 to 11 could also be used to find the value of every element in the array. However, although that technique would work in this situation, the keys in an array may not always be sequential and, as you will see in the next section, may not even be numeric.

Associative Arrays

The array examples so far in this chapter have used numeric keys. An *associative* array allows you to use textual keys so that the indexes can be more descriptive.

To assign a value to an array by using an associative key and to reference that value, you simply use a textual key name enclosed in quotes, as in the following examples:

```
$temps["jan"] = 38;
echo $temps["jan"];
```

To define the complete array of average monthly temperatures in this way, you can use the array function as before, but you indicate the key value as well as each element. You use the => symbol to show the relationship between a key and its value:

```
$temps = array("jan" => 38, "feb" => 40, "mar" => 49,
               "apr" => 60, "may" => 70, "jun" => 79,
               "jul" => 84, "aug" => 83, "sep" => 76,
               "oct" => 65, "nov" => 54, "dec" => 42);
```

The elements in an associative array are stored in the order in which they are defined (you will learn about sorting arrays later in this lesson), and traversing this array in a loop will find the elements in the order defined. You can call print_r on the array to verify this. The first few lines of output are as follows:

```
Array
(
    [jan] => 38
    [feb] => 40
    [mar] => 49
...
```

Array Functions

You have already seen the array function used to generate an array from a list of values. Now let's take a look at some of the other functions PHP provides for manipulating arrays.

There are many more array functions in PHP than this book can cover. If you need to perform a complex array operation that you have not learned about, refer to the online documentation at www.php.net/ref.array.

Sorting

To sort the values in an array, you use the `sort` function or one of its derivatives, as in the following example:

```
sort($temps);
```

> **Sorting Functions** `sort` and other related functions take a single array argument and sort that array. The sorted array is not returned; the return value indicates success or failure.

Sorting the original `$temps` array with `sort` arranges the values into numeric order, but the key values are also renumbered. After you perform the sort, index 0 of the array will contain the lowest value from the array, and there is no way of telling which value corresponds to each month.

You can use `asort` to sort an array while maintaining the key associations, whether it is an associative array or numerically indexed. After you sort `$temps`, index 0 will still contain January's average temperature, but if you loop through the array, the elements will be retrieved in sorted order.

Using the associative array `$temps` as an example, the following code displays the months and their average temperatures, from coldest to hottest:

```
$temps = array("jan" => 38, "feb" => 40, "mar" => 49,
               "apr" => 60, "may" => 70, "jun" => 79,
               "jul" => 84, "aug" => 83, "sep" => 76,
               "oct" => 65, "nov" => 54, "dec" => 42);
asort($temps);
foreach($temps as $month => $temp) {
  print "$month: $temp <br>\n";
}
```

It is also possible to sort an array on the keys rather than on the element values, by using `ksort`. Using `ksort` on the associative `$temps` array arranges the elements alphabetically on the month name keys. Therefore, when you loop through the sorted array, the first value fetched would be `$temps["apr"]`, followed by `$temps["aug"]`, and so on.

To reverse the sort order for any of these functions, you use rsort in place of sort. The reverse of asort is arsort, and the reverse of ksort is krsort. To reverse the order of an array as it stands without sorting, you simply use array_reverse.

Randomizing an Array

As well as sorting the values of an array into order, PHP provides functions so that you can easily randomize elements in an array.

The shuffle function works in a similar way to the sorting functions: It takes a single array argument and shuffles the elements in that array into a random order. As with sort, the key associations are lost, and the shuffled values will always be indexed numerically.

Set Functions

By treating an array as a set of values, you can perform set arithmetic by using PHP's array functions.

To combine the values from different arrays (a union operation), you use the array_merge function with two or more array arguments, as in the following example:

```
$union = array_merge($array1, $array2, $array3, ...);
```

A new array is returned that contains all the elements from the listed arrays. In this example, the $union array will contain all the elements in $array1, followed by all the elements in $array2, and so on.

To remove duplicate values from any array, you use array_unique so that if two different index keys refer to the same value, only one will be kept.

The array_intersect function performs an intersection on two arrays. The following example produces a new array, $intersect, that contains all the elements from $array1 that are also present in $array2:

```
$intersect = array_intersect($array1, $array2);
```

To find the difference between two sets, you can use the `array_diff` function. The following example returns the array `$diff`, which contains only elements from `$array1` that are not present in `$array2`:

```
$diff = array_diff($array1, $array2);
```

Looking Inside Arrays

The `count` function returns the number of elements in an array. It takes a single array argument. For example, the following statement shows that there are 12 values in the `$temps` array:

```
echo count($temps);
```

To find out whether a value exists within an array without having to write a loop to search through every value, you can use `in_array` or `array_search`. The first argument is the value to search for, and the second is the array to look inside:

```
if (in_array("PHP", $languages)) {
  ...
}
```

The difference between these functions is the return value. If the value exists within the array, `array_search` returns the corresponding key, whereas `in_array` returns only a Boolean result.

> **Needle in a Haystack**   Somewhat confusingly, the order of the *needle* and *haystack* arguments to `in_array` and `array_search` is opposite that of string functions, such as `strpos` and `strstr`.

To check whether a particular key exists in an array, you use `array_key_exists`. The following example determines whether the December value of `$temps` has been set:

```
if (array_key_exists("dec", $temps)) {
  ...
}
```

Serializing

The serialize function creates a textual representation of the data an array holds. This is a powerful feature that gives you the ability to easily write the contents of a PHP array to a database or file.

Lessons 17, "Filesystem Access," and 19, "Using a MySQL Database," deal with the specifics of filesystem and database storage. For now let's just take a look at how serialization of an array works.

Calling serialize with an array argument returns a string that represents the keys and values in that array, in a structured format. You can then decode that string by using the unserialize function to return the original array.

The serialized string that represents the associative array $temps is as follows:

```
a:12:{s:3:"jan";i:38;s:3:"feb";i:40;s:3:"mar";i:49;
s:3:"apr";i:60; s:3:"may";i:70;s:3:"jun";
i:79;s:3:"jul";i:84;s:3:"aug";i:83;s:3:"sep";
si:76;s:3:"oct";i:65;s:3:"nov";i:54;s:3:"dec";i:42;}
```

You can probably figure out how this string is structured, and the only argument you would ever pass to unserialize is the result of a serialize operation—there is no point in trying to construct it yourself.

Multidimensional Arrays

It is possible—and often very useful—to use arrays to store two-dimensional or even multidimensional data.

Accessing Two-Dimensional Data

In fact, a *two-dimensional array* is an array of arrays. Suppose you were to use an array to store the average monthly temperature, by year, using two key dimensions—the month and the year. You might display the average temperature from February 1995 as follows:

```
echo $temps[1995]["feb"];
```

Because $temps is an array of arrays, $temps[1995] is an array of temper-atures, indexed by month, and you can reference its elements by adding the key name in square brackets.

Defining a Multidimensional Array

Defining a multidimensional array is fairly straightforward, as long as you remember that what you are working with is actually an array that contains more arrays.

You can initialize values by using references to the individual elements, as follows:

```
$temps[1995]["feb"] = 41;
```

You can also define multidimensional arrays by nesting the array function in the appropriate places. The following example defines the first few months for three years (the full array would clearly be much larger than this):

```
$temps = array (
    1995 => array ("jan" => 36, "feb" => 42, "mar" => 51),
    1996 => array ("jan" => 37, "feb" => 42, "mar" => 49),
    1997 => array ("jan" => 34, "feb" => 40, "mar" => 50) );
```

The print_r function can follow as many dimensions as an array con-tains, and the formatted output will be indented to make each level of the hierarchy readable. The following is the output from the three-dimensional $temps array just defined:

```
Array
(
    [1995] => Array
        (
            [jan] => 36
            [feb] => 42
            [mar] => 51
        )

    [1996] => Array
        (
            [jan] => 37
            [feb] => 42
```

```
            [mar] => 49
        )

    [1997] => Array
        (
            [jan] => 34
            [feb] => 40
            [mar] => 50
        )

)
```

Summary

In this lesson you have learned how to create arrays of data and manipulate them. The next lesson examines how regular expressions are used to perform pattern matching on strings.

LESSON 8
Regular Expressions

In this lesson you will learn about advanced string manipulation using regular expressions. You will see how to use regular expressions to validate a string and to perform a search-and-replace operation.

Introducing Regular Expressions

Using regular expressions—sometimes known as *regex*—is a powerful and concise way of writing a rule that identifies a particular string format. Because they can express quite complex rules in only a few characters, if you have not come across them before, regular expressions can look very confusing indeed.

At its very simplest, a regular expression can be just a character string, where the expression matches any string that contains those characters in sequence. At a more advanced level, a regular expression can identify detailed patterns of characters within a string and break a string into components based on those patterns.

Types of Regular Expression

PHP supports two different types of regular expressions: the POSIX-extended syntax—which is examined in this lesson—and the Perl-Compatible Regular Expression (PCRE). Both types perform the same function, using a different syntax, and there is really no need to know how to use both types. If you are already familiar with Perl, you may find it easier to use the PCRE functions than to learn the POSIX syntax.

Documentation for PCRE can be found online at www.php.net/manual/en/ref.pcre.php.

Using `ereg`

The `ereg` function in PHP is used to test a string against a regular expression. Using a very simple regex, the following example checks whether $phrase contains the substring PHP:

```php
$phrase = "I love PHP";
if (ereg("PHP", $phrase)) {
  echo "The expression matches";
}
```

If you run this script through your web browser, you will see that the expression does indeed match $phrase.

Regular expressions are case-sensitive, so if the expression were in lowercase, this example would not find a match. To perform a non-case-sensitive regex comparison, you can use `eregi`:

```php
if (eregi("php", $phrase)) {
  echo "The expression matches";
}
```

> **Performance** The regular expressions you have seen so far perform basic string matching that can also be performed by the functions you learned about in Lesson 6, "Working with Strings," such as `strstr`. In general, a script will perform better if you use string functions in place of `ereg` for simple string comparisons.

Testing Sets of Characters

As well as checking that a sequence of characters appears in a string, you can test for a set of characters by enclosing them in square brackets. You simply list all the characters you want to test, and the expression matches if any one of them occurs.

The following example is actually equivalent to the use of `eregi` shown earlier in this lesson:

```
if (ereg("[Pp][Hh][Pp]", $phrase)) {
  echo "The expression matches";
}
```

This expression checks for either an uppercase or lowercase *P*, followed by an uppercase or lowercase *H*, followed by an uppercase or lowercase *P*.

You can also specify a range of characters by using a hyphen between two letters or numbers. For example, [A-Z] would match any uppercase letter, and [0-4] would match any number between zero and four.

The following condition is true only if $phrase contains at least one uppercase letter:

```
if (ereg("[A-Z]", $phrase)) ...
```

The ^ symbol can be used to negate a set so that the regular expression specifies that the string must not contain a set of characters. The following condition is true only if $phrase contains at least one non-numeric character:

```
if (ereg("[^0-9]", $phrase)) ...
```

Common Character Classes

You can use a number of sets of characters when using regex. To test for all alphanumeric characters, you would need a regular expression that looks like this:

```
[A-Za-z0-9]
```

The character class that represents the same set of characters can be represented in a much clearer fashion:

```
[[:alnum:]]
```

The [: and :] characters indicate that the expression contains the name of a character class. The available classes are shown in Table 8.1.

TABLE 8.1   Character Classes for Use in Regular Expressions

Class Name	Description
alnum	All alphanumeric characters, A–Z, a–z, and 0–9
alpha	All letters, A–Z and a–z
digit	All digits, 0–9
lower	All lowercase characters, a–z
print	All printable characters, including space
punct	All punctuation characters—any printable character that is not a space or alnum
space	All whitespace characters, including tabs and newlines
upper	All uppercase letters, A–Z

Testing for Position

All the expressions you have seen so far find a match if that expression appears anywhere within the compared string. You can also test for position within a string in a regular expression.

The ^ character, when not part of a character class, indicates the start of the string, and $ indicates the end of the string. You could use the following conditions to check whether $phrase begins or ends with an alphabetic character, respectively:

```
if (ereg("^[a-z]", $phrase)) ...
```

```
if (ereg("[a-z]$", $phrase)) ...
```

If you want to check that a string contains only a particular pattern, you can sandwich that pattern between ^ and $. For example, the following condition checks that $number contains only a single numeric digit:

```
if (ereg("^[[:digit:]]$", $number) ...
```

The Dollar Sign   If you want to look for a literal $
character in a regular expression, you must delimit the
character as \$ so that it is not treated as the end-of-
line indicator.

When your expression is in double quotes, you must
use \\$ to double-delimit the character; otherwise, the
$ sign may be interpreted as the start of a variable
identifier.

Wildcard Matching

The dot or period (.) character in a regular expression is a wildcard—it
matches any character at all. For example, the following condition
matches any four-letter word that contains a double *o*:

```
if (ereg("^.oo.$", $word)) ...
```

The ^ and $ characters indicate the start and end of the string, and each
dot can be any character. This expression would match the words *book*
and *tool*, but not *buck* or *stool*.

Wildcards   A regular expression that simply contains
a dot matches any string that contains at least one
character. You must use the ^ and $ characters to indi-
cate length limits on the expression.

Repeating Patterns

You have now seen how to test for a particular character or for a set or
class of characters within a string, as well as how to use the wildcard
character to define a wide range of patterns in a regular expression. Along
with these, you can use another set of characters to indicate where a pattern can or must be repeated a number of times within a string.

You can use an asterisk (*) to indicate that the preceding item can appear zero or more times in the string, and you can use a plus (+) symbol to ensure that the item appears at least once.

The following examples, which use the * and + characters, are very similar to one another. They both match a string of any length that contains only alphanumeric characters. However, the first condition also matches an empty string because the asterisk denotes zero or more occurrences of [[:alnum::]]:

```
if (ereg("^[[:alnum:]]*$", $phrase)) ...

if (ereg("^[[:alnum:]]+$", $phrase)) ...
```

To denote a group of matching characters that should repeat, you use parentheses around them. For example, the following condition matches a string of any even length that contains alternating letters and numbers:

```
if (ereg("^([[:alpha:]][[:digit:]])+$", $string)) ...
```

This example uses the plus symbol to indicate that the letter/number sequence could repeat one or more times. To specify a fixed number of times to repeat, the number can be given in braces. A single number or a comma-separated range can be given, as in the following example:

```
if (ereg("^([[:alpha:]][[:digit:]]){2,3}$", $string)) ...
```

This expression would match four or six character strings that contain alternating letters and numbers. However, a single letter and number or a longer combination would not match.

The question mark (?) character indicates that the preceding item may appear either once or not at all. The same behavior could be achieved by using {0,1} to specify the number of times to repeat a pattern.

Some Practical Examples

You use regex mostly to validate user input in scripts, to make sure that a value entered is acceptable. The following are some practical examples of using regular expressions.

Zip Codes

If you have a customer's zip code stored in $zip, you might want to check that it has a valid format. A U.S. zip code always consists of five numeric digits, and it can optionally be followed by a hyphen and four more digits. The following condition validates a zip code in this format:

```
if (ereg("^[[:digit:]]{5}(-[[:digit:]]{4})?$", $zip)) ...
```

The first part of this regular expression ensures that $zip begins with five numeric digits. The second part is in parentheses and followed by a question mark, indicating that this part is optional. The second part is defined as a hyphen character followed by four digits.

Regardless of whether the second part appears, the $ symbol indicates the end of the string, so there can be no other characters other than those allowed by the expression if this condition is to be satisfied. Therefore, this condition matches a zip code that looks like either 90210 or 90210-1234.

Telephone Numbers

You might want to enforce the format of a telephone number to ensure that it looks like (555)555-5555. There are no optional parts to this format. However, because the parentheses characters have a special meaning for regex, they have to be escaped with a backslash.

The following condition validates a telephone number in this format:

```
if (ereg("^\([[:digit:]]{3}\)[[:digit:]]{3}-[[:digit:]]{4}$",
         $telephone)) ...
```

Email Addresses

You need to consider many variables when validating an email address. At the very simplest level, an email address for a .com domain name looks like somename@somedomain.com.

However, there are many variations, including top-level domain names that are two characters, such as .ca, or four characters, such as .info.

Some country-specific domains have a two-part extension, such as .co.uk or .com.au.

As you can see, a regular expression rule to validate an email address needs to be quite forgiving. However, by making some general assumptions about the format of an email address, you can still create a rule that rejects many badly formed addresses.

There are two main parts to an email address, and they are separated by an @ symbol. The characters that can appear to the left of the @ symbol—usually the recipient's mailbox name—can be alphanumeric and can contain certain symbols.

Let's assume that the mailbox part of an email address can consist of any characters except for the @ symbol itself and can be any length. Rather than try to list all the acceptable characters you can think of—for instance, should you allow an apostrophe in an email address?—it is usually good enough to enforce that email address can contain only one @ character and that anything up to that character is a valid mailbox name.

For the regex rule, you can define that the domain part of an email address consists of two or more parts, separated by dots. You can also assume that the last part may only be between two and four characters in length, which is sufficient for all top-level domain names currently in use.

The set of characters that can be used in parts of the domain is more restrictive than the mailbox name—only lowercase alphanumeric characters and a hyphen can be used.

Taking these assumptions into consideration, you can come up with the following condition to test the validity of an email address:

```
if (ereg("^[^@]+@([a-z0-9\-]+\.)+[a-z]{2,4}$", $email)) ...
```

This regular expression breaks down as follows: any number of characters followed by an @ symbol, followed by one or more parts consisting of only lowercase letters, numbers, or a hyphen. Each of those parts ends with a dot, and the final part must be between two and four letters in length.

> **How Far to Go**   This expression could be even further
> refined. For instance, a domain name cannot begin
> with a hyphen and has a maximum length of 63 char-
> acters. However, for the purpose of catching mistyped
> email addresses, this expression is more than
> sufficient.

Breaking a String into Components

You have used parentheses to group together parts of a regular expression
to indicate a repeating pattern. You can also use parentheses to indicate
subparts of an expression, and ereg allows you to break a pattern into
components based on the parentheses.

When an optional third argument is passed to ereg, that variable is
assigned an array of values that correspond to the parts of the pattern
identified by the parentheses in the regular expression.

Let's use the email address regular expression as an example. The following code includes three sets of parentheses to isolate the mailbox name,
domain name (apart from the extension), and domain extension:

```
$email = "chris@lightwood.net";
if (ereg("^([^@]+)@([a-z\-]+\.)+([a-z]{2,4})$",
              $email, $match)) {
  echo "Mailbox: " . $match[1] . "<br>";
  echo "Domain name: " . $match[2] . "<br>";
  echo "Domain type: " . $match[3] . "<br>";
}
else {
  echo "Email address is invalid";
}
```

If you run this script in a web browser, you get output similar to the following:

```
Mailbox: chris
Domain name: lightwood.
Domain type: net
```

Note that the first key of $match refers to the first pattern found. The array keys are numbered from zero, as usual; however, $match[0] contains the entire matched pattern.

Searching and Replacing

You can use regular expressions to perform search and replace operations on a string with the ereg_replace function. Its three arguments are a regex search pattern, the replacement string, and the string to replace into. The modified string is returned.

> str_replace If you want to perform a simple string replace operation that does not require a regular expression, you can use str_replace instead of ereg_replace. str_replace is more efficient because PHP does not even have to consider that you might be looking for a regular expression.

For example, to blank out a telephone number before displaying a string, you could use the following:

```
echo ereg_replace(
        "\([[:digit:]]{3}\)[[:digit:]]{3}-[[:digit:]]{4}$",
        "(XXX)XXX-XXXX", $string);
```

Just like you can use eregi in place of ereg, to perform a non-case-sensitive search and replace using regex, you can use eregi_replace.

Summary

In this lesson you have learned the basics of regular expressions. If you want to find out more, you can refer to *Sams Teach Yourself Regular Expressions in 10 Minutes* by Ben Forta.

In the next lesson you will learn how to handle date and time values in PHP.

LESSON 9

Working with Dates and Times

In this lesson you will learn how to store, display, and manipulate date and time values in PHP.

Date Formats

PHP does not have a native date data type, so in order to store date values in a script, you must first decide on the best way to store these values.

Do-It-Yourself Date Formats

Although you often see dates written in a structured format, such as 05/03/1974 or 2001-12-31, these are not ideal formats for working with date values. However, the latter of these two is more suitable than the first because the order of its components is from most significant (the year) to the least significant (the day), so values can be compared using the usual PHP operators.

As a string, 2002-01-01 is greater than 2001-12-31, but because comparisons are performed more efficiently on numbers than on strings, this could be written better as just 20020201, where the format is YYYYMMDD. This format can be extended to include a time portion—again, with the most significant elements first—as YYYYMMDDHHMMSS, for example.

However, date arithmetic with this format is nearly impossible. While you can add one to 20040501, for instance, and find the next day in that month, simply adding one to 20030531 would result in a nonsense date of May 32.

Unix Timestamp Format

The Unix timestamp format is an integer representation of a date and time. It is a value that counts the number of seconds since midnight on January 1, 1970.

 The Unix Epoch   A timestamp with integer value zero represents precisely midnight, Greenwich Mean Time (GMT), on January 1, 1970. This date is known as the *Unix Epoch*.

Right now, we have a 10-digit date and time timestamp. To find the current timestamp, you use the `time` function:

```
echo time();
```

The Unix timestamp format is useful because it is very easy to perform calculations on because you know that the value always represents a number of seconds. For example, you can just add 3,600 to a timestamp value to increase the time by one hour or add 86,400 to add one day—because there are 3,600 seconds in an hour and 86,400 seconds in a day.

One drawback, however, is that the Unix timestamp format cannot handle dates prior to 1970. Although some systems may be able to use a negative timestamp value to count backward from the Epoch, this behavior cannot be relied on.

Timestamps are good for representing contemporary date values, but they may not always be suitable for handling dates of birth or dates of historical significance. You should consider what values you will be working with when deciding whether a timestamp is the correct format to use.

Timestamp Limitations   The maximum value of a Unix timestamp depends on the system's architecture. Most systems use a 32-bit integer to store a timestamp, making the latest time it can represent 3:14am on January 19, 2038.

Working with Timestamps

There are times when using your own date format is beneficial, but in most cases a timestamp is the best choice. Let's look at how PHP interacts with the timestamp date format.

Formatting Dates

In Lesson 1, "Getting to Know PHP," you used the date function to display the current date by passing a format string as the argument, such as in the following example:

```
echo date("j F Y H:i:s");
```

The date displayed looks something like this:

```
12 November 2004 10:23:55
```

The optional second argument to date is a timestamp value of the date that you want to display. For example, to display the date when a timestamp first requires a 10-digit number, you could use the following:

```
echo date("j F Y H:I:s", 1000000000);
```

The list of format codes for the date function is shown in Table 9.1.

TABLE 9.1   Format Codes for date

Code	Description
a	Lowercase am or pm
A	Uppercase AM or PM
d	Two-digit day of month, 01–31
D	Three-letter day name, Mon–Sun
F	Full month name, January–December
g	12-hour hour with no leading zero, 1–12
G	24-hour hour with no leading zero, 0–23
h	12-hour hour with leading zero, 01–12

Code	Description
H	24-hour hour with leading zero, 00–23
I	Minutes with leading zero, 00–59
j	Day of month with no leading zero, 1–31
l	Full day name, Monday–Sunday
m	Month number with leading zeros, 01–12
M	Three letter month name, Jan–Dec
n	Month number with no leading zeros, 1–12
s	Seconds with leading zero, 00–59
S	Ordinal suffix for day of month, st, nd, rd, or th
w	Number of day of week, 0–6, where 0 is Sunday
W	Week number, 0–53
y	Two-digit year number
Y	Four-digit year number
z	Day of year, 0–365

Creating Timestamps

Don't worry; you don't have to count from January 1, 1970, each time you want to calculate a timestamp. The PHP function mktime returns a timestamp based on given date and time values.

The arguments, in order, are the hour, minute, second, month, day, and year. The following example would assign $timestamp the timestamp value for 8 a.m. on December 25, 2001:

```
$timestamp = mktime(8, 0, 0, 12, 25, 2001);
```

The Unix timestamp format counts from January 1, 1970, at midnight GMT. The mktime function returns a timestamp relative to the time zone in which your system operates. For instance, mktime would return a timestamp value 3,600 higher when running on a web server in Texas than on a machine in New York with the same arguments.

Daylight Saving Time If you are only concerned with the date part of a timestamp, the first three arguments to mktime only matter if they are close to midnight at a time of the year when daylight saving time is a factor.

For instance, when the clocks are moved back one hour, that day is only 23 hours long. Adding 86,400 seconds to a timestamp that represents midnight on that day will actually move the day part of the timestamp forward two days. You can use midday instead of midnight as the time element to avoid these issues.

Greenwich Mean Time To obtain timestamp values that are always relative to GMT—the time in London when there is no daylight saving time adjustment— you use gmmktime instead of mktime.

The mktime function is forgiving if you supply it with nonsense arguments, such as a day of the month that doesn't exist. For instance, if you try to calculate a timestamp for February 29 in a non-leap year, the value returned will actually represent March 1, as the following statement confirms:

```
echo date("d/m/Y", mktime(12, 0, 0, 2, 29, 2003));
```

You can exploit this behavior as a way of performing date and time arithmetic. Consider the following example, which calculates and displays the date and time 37 hours after midday on December 30, 2001:

```
$time = mktime(12 + 37, 0, 0, 12, 30, 2001);
echo date("d/m/Y H:i:s", $time);
```

By simply adding a constant to one of the arguments in `mktime`, you can shift the timestamp value returned by that amount. The date and time display as follows:

```
01/01/2002 01:00:00
```

The value returned in this example has correctly shifted the day, month, year, and hour values, taking into account the number of days in December and that December is the last month of the year.

Converting Other Date Formats to Timestamps

If you have a date stored in a format like DD-MM-YYYY, it's a fairly simple process to convert this to a timestamp by breaking up the string around the hyphen character. The `explode` function takes a delimiter argument and a string and returns an array that contains each part of the string that was separated by the given delimiter.

The following example breaks a date in this format into its components and builds a timestamp from those values:

```
$date = "03-05-1974";
$parts = explode("/", $date);
$timestamp = mktime(12, 0, 0,
                    $parts[1], $parts[0], $parts[2]);
```

For many date formats, there is an even easier way to create a timestamp—using the function `strtotime`. The following examples all display the same valid timestamp from a string date value:

```
$timestamp = strtotime("3 May 04");
$timestamp = strtotime("3rd May 2004");
$timestamp = strtotime("May 3, 2004");
$timestamp = strtotime("3-may-04");
$timestamp = strtotime("2004-05-03");
$timestamp = strtotime("05/03/2004");
```

Note that in the last examples, the date format given is MM/DD/YYYY, not DD/MM/YYYY. You can find the complete list of formats that are acceptable to `strtotime` at www.gnu.org/software/tar/manual/html_chapter/tar_7.html.

Getting Information About a Timestamp

You can use the date function to return part or all of the date that a timestamp represents as a formatted string, but PHP also provides the getdate function, which returns useful values from a timestamp.

Taking a single timestamp argument, getdate returns an associative array that contains the indexes shown in Table 9.2.

TABLE 9.2   Key Elements Returned by getdate

Key	Description
seconds	Seconds, 0–59
minutes	Minutes, 0–59
hours	Hours, 0–23
mday	Day of the month, 0–31
wday	Day of the week, 0–6, where 0 is Sunday
yday	Day of the year, 0–365
mon	Month number, 0–12
year	Four-digit year number
weekday	Full day name, Sunday–Saturday
month	Full month name, January–December

The following example uses getdate to determine whether the current date falls on a weekday or weekend:

```
$now = getdate();
switch ($now[wday]) {
  case 0:  // Sunday
  case 6:  // Saturday
           echo "It's the weekend";
           break;
  default: echo "It's a weekday";
}
```

Note that when getdate is called without a timestamp argument, it returns an array that contains the elements in Table 9.2 for the current time.

Summary

In this lesson you have learned how to store and manipulate date and time values in PHP. In the next lesson you will learn about classes in PHP, and you will discover how to use third-party library classes that you download.

LESSON 10
Using Classes

In this lesson you will learn the basics of object-oriented PHP. You will see how a class is defined and how you can access methods and properties from third-party classes.

Object-Oriented PHP

PHP can, if you want, be written in an object-oriented (OO) fashion. In PHP5, the OO functionality of the language has been enhanced considerably.

If you are familiar with other OO languages, such as C++ or Java, you may prefer the OO approach to programming PHP, whereas if you are used to other procedural languages, you may not want to use objects at all. There are, after all, many ways to solve the same problem.

If you are new to programming as well as to PHP, you probably have no strong feelings either way just yet. It's certainly true that OO concepts are easier to grasp if you have no programming experience at all than if you have a background in a procedural language, but even so OO methods are not something that can be taught in a ten-minute lesson in this book!

The aim of this lesson is to introduce how a class is created and referenced in PHP so that if you have a preference for using objects, you can begin to develop scripts by using OO methods. Most importantly, however, you will be able to pick up and use some of the many freely available third-party class libraries that are available for PHP from resources such as those at www.phpclasses.org, and those that are part of PEAR, which you will learn about in Lesson 25, "Using PEAR."

What Is a Class?

A *class* is the template structure that defines an object. It can contain *functions*—also known as *class methods*—and *variables*—also known as *class properties* or *attributes*.

Each class consists of a set of PHP statements that define how to perform a task or set of tasks that you want to repeat frequently. The class can contain *private* methods, which are only used internally to perform the class's functions, and *public* methods, which you can use to interface with the class.

A good class hides its inner workings and includes only the public methods that are required to provide a simple interface to its functionality. If you bundle complex blocks of programming into a class, any script that uses that class does not need to worry about exactly how a particular operation is performed. All that is required is knowledge of the class's public methods.

Because there are many freely available third-party classes for PHP, in many situations, you need not waste time implementing a feature in PHP that is already freely available.

When to Use Classes

At first, there may not appear to be any real advantage in using a class over using functions that have been modularized into an include file. OO is not necessarily a better approach to programming; rather, it is a different way of thinking. Whether you choose to develop your own classes is a matter of preference.

One of the advantages of OO programming is that it can allow your code to scale into very large projects easily. In OO programming, a class can inherit the properties of another and extend it; this means that functionality that has already been developed can be reused and adapted to fit a particular situation. This is called *inheritance*, and it is a key feature of OO development.

When you have completed this book, if you are interested in learning more about OO programming, take a look at *Sams Teach Yourself Object-Oriented Programming in 21 Days* by Anthony Sintes.

What a Class Looks Like

A class is a grouping of various functions and variables—and that is exactly how it looks when written in PHP. A class definition looks very similar to a function definition; it begins with the keyword class and an identifier, followed by the class definition, contained in a pair of curly brackets ({}).

The following is a trivial example of a class to show how a class looks. This example contains just one property, myValue, and one method, myMethod (which does nothing):

```
class myClass {
  var $myValue;

  function myMethod() {
    return 0;
  }
}
```

If you are already familiar with OO programming and want to get a head start with OO PHP, you can refer to the online documentation at www.php.net/manual/en/language.oop5.php.

Creating and Using Objects

To create an instance of an object from a class, you use the new keyword in PHP, as follows:

```
$myObject = new myClass;
```

In this example, myClass is the name of a class that must be defined in the script—usually in an include file—and $myObject becomes a myClass object.

> ✏️ **Multiple Objects** You can use the same class many times in the same script by simply creating new instances from that class but with new object names.

Methods and Properties

The methods and properties defined in myClass can be referenced for $myObject. The following are generic examples:

```
$myObject->myValue = "555-1234";
$myObject->myMethod();
```

The arrow symbol (->)—made up of a hyphen and greater-than symbol—indicates a method or property of the given object. To reference the current object within the class definition, you use the special name $this.

The following example defines myClass with a method that references one of the object properties:

```
class myClass {
  var $myValue = "Jelly";

  function myMethod() {
    echo "myValue is " . $this->myValue . "<br>";
  }
}

$myObject    new myClass;
$myObject->myMethod();
$myObject->myValue = "Custard";
$myObject->myMethod();
```

This example makes two separate calls to myMethod. The first time it displays the default value of myValue; an assignment within the class specifies a default value for a property. The second call comes after that property has had a new value assigned. The class uses $this to reference its own property and does not care, or even know, that in the script its name is $myObject.

If the class includes a special method known as a *constructor*, arguments can be supplied in parentheses when an object is created, and those values are later passed to the constructor function. This is usually done to initialize a set of properties for each object instance, and it looks similar to the following:

```
$myObject = new myClass($var1, $var2);
```

Using a Third-Party Class

The best way to learn how to work with classes is to use one. Let's take a look at a popular third-party class written by Manuel Lemos, which provides a comprehensive way to validate email addresses. You can download this class from www.phpclasses.org/browse/file/28.html and save the file locally as email_validation.php.

Manuel's class validates an email address not only by checking that its format is correct but also by performing a domain name lookup to ensure that it can be delivered. It even connects to the remote mail server to make sure the given mailbox actually exists.

> **Domain Lookups**   If you are following this example on a Windows-based web server, you need to download an additional file, getmxrr.php, to add a suitable domain name lookup function to PHP. You can download this file from www.phpclasses.org/browse/file/2080.html.

The email_validation.php script defines a class called email_validation_class, so you first need to create a new instance of a validator object called $validator, as follows:

```
$validator = new email_validation_class;
```

You can set a number of properties for your new class. Some are required in order for the class to work properly, and others allow you to change the default behavior.

Each object instance requires you to set the properties that contain the mailbox and domain parts of a real email address, which is the address that will be given to the remote mail server when checking a mailbox. There are no default values for these properties; they always have to be set as follows:

```
$validator->localuser = "chris";
$validator->localhost = "lightwood.net";
```

The optional `timeout` property defines how many seconds to wait when connected to a remote mail server before giving up. Setting the `debug` property causes the text of the communication with the remote server to be displayed onscreen. You never need to do this, though, unless you are interested in what is going on. The following statements define a timeout of 10 seconds and turn on debug output:

```
$validator->timeout = 10;
$validator->debug = TRUE;
```

The full list of adjustable properties for a validator object is shown in Table 10.1.

TABLE 10.1 Properties of an `email_validation_class` Object

Property	Description
timeout	Indicates the number of seconds before timing out when connecting to a destination mail server
data_timeout	Indicates the number of seconds before timing out while data is exchanged with the mail server; if zero, takes the value of `timeout`
localuser	Indicates the user part of the email address of the sending user
localhost	Indicates the domain part of the email address of the sending user
debug	Indicates whether to output the text of the communication with the mail server
html_debug	Indicates whether the debug output should be formatted as an HTML page

The methods in email_validation_class are mostly private; you cannot call them directly, but the internal code is made up of a set of functions. If you examine email_validation.php, you will see function definitions, including Tokenize, GetLine, and VerifyResultLines, but none of these are useful outside the object itself.

The only public method in a validator object is named ValidateEmailBox, and when called, it initiates the email address validation of a string argument. The following example shows how ValidateEmailBox is called:

```
$email = "chris@datasnake.co.uk";
if ($validator->ValidateEmailBox($email)) {
  echo "$email is a valid email address";
}
else {
  echo "$email could not be validated";
}
```

The return value from ValidateEmailBox indicates whether the validation check is successful. If you have turned on the debug attribute, you will also see output similar to the following, in addition to the output from the script:

```
Resolving host name "mail.datasnake.co.uk"...
Connecting to host address "217.158.68.125"...
Connected.
S 220 mail.datasnake.co.uk ESMTP
C HELO lightwood.net
S 250 mail.datasnake.co.uk
C MAIL FROM: <chris@lightwood.net>
S 250 ok
C RCPT TO: <chris@datasnake.co.uk>
S 250 ok
C DATA
S 354 go ahead
This host states that the address is valid.
Disconnected.
```

Summary

In this lesson you have learned about OO PHP and seen how to use classes in your own scripts. In the next lesson you will learn how PHP can interact with HTML forms.

LESSON 11
Processing HTML Forms

The reason that PHP came into existence was to provide a simple way of processing user-submitted data in HTML forms. In this lesson you will learn how data entered in each type of form input is made available in a PHP script.

Submitting a Form to PHP

In case you are not familiar with HTML forms at all, let's begin by looking over what is involved in creating a web page that can collect information from a user and submit it to a web script.

The <FORM> Tag

The HTML <FORM> tag indicates an area of a web page that, when it contains text-entry fields or other form input elements, submits the values entered by a user to a particular URL.

The ACTION attribute in a <FORM> tag indicates the location of the script that the values are to be passed to. It can be a location relative to the current page or a full URL that begins with http://.

The METHOD attribute indicates the way in which the user's web browser will bundle up the data to be sent. Two methods, GET and POST, vary visibly only slightly. Form data submitted using the GET method is tagged on to the end of the URL, whereas the POST method sends the data to the web server without its being visible.

> **The GET Method**   You have probably seen URLs with
> GET method data attached, even if you didn't know
> that's what was going on. If you've ever use the
> search box at a website and the page address has
> come back with ?search=yourword, it submitted the
> form by using the GET method.

In most situations where you are using an HTML form, the POST method
is preferable. It is not only better aesthetically—because the submitted
values are not revealed in the script URL—but there is no limit on the
amount of data that can be submitted in this way. The amount of data that
can be submitted by using the GET method is limited by the maximum
URL length that a web browser can handle (the limit in Internet Explorer
is 2,048 characters) and the HTTP version on the server (HTTP/1.0 must
allow at least 256 characters, whereas HTTP/1.1 must allow at least
2,048).

The <INPUT> Tag

The <INPUT> tag is used to add one of several types of form input to a
web page. The type of input item is specified in the TYPE attribute, and the
simplest type is a TEXT input item.

To create a TEXT input item that is suitable for entering a user's email
address, you could use the following HTML:

```
<INPUT TYPE="TEXT" NAME="name" SIZE="30" VALUE="">
```

In this HTML, you supply an empty VALUE attribute because you do not
want to supply a default value for the input; however, the VALUE attribute
can be omitted.

> **Field Lengths**   The display size of a field does not
> affect how PHP handles the submitted values. This
> input has a display size of 30 characters but no
> MAXLENGTH attribute is set, so users with unusually long
> names can still type beyond the length of the field.

The CHECKBOX input type creates an input item that has only two possible values: on and off. Check boxes are useful for true/false values, and you could use the following HTML to create a check box with which the user could indicate whether he minds us contacting him by email:

```
<INPUT TYPE="CHECKBOX" NAME="may_contact" VALUE="Y" CHECKED>
```

In this case, the CHECKED attribute indicates that the check box should be checked automatically when the page loads.

The RADIO type is similar to a check box, but instead of a true/false value, a radio button group can contain several values, of which only one can be selected at a time.

To create a radio button group that can be used to gather the user's gender, you could use the following:

```
<INPUT TYPE="radio" NAME="gender" VALUE="m"> Male
<INPUT TYPE="radio" NAME="gender" VALUE="f"> Female
```

> **Naming Radio Buttons**   The NAME attribute determines the grouping of radio buttons. Only one selection can be made for each radio button group, although you can have several radio button groups on a page if you want. In this example, both buttons have the same name, gender.

To indicate that one of the buttons in a radio button group should be preselected, you can use the CHECKED attribute. For instance, if you are creating a website that will appeal primarily to women, you can pre-select the female option, as follows:

```
<INPUT TYPE="radio" NAME="gender" VALUE="m"> Male
<INPUT TYPE="radio" NAME="gender" VALUE="f" CHECKED> Female
```

The final input type that you will learn about is the SUBMIT button. This is the button you click to send the contents of a form to the script specified in the form's METHOD attribute. The label on the button is specified in the

VALUE attribute, so the following HTML would create a submit button labeled Send comments:

```
<INPUT TYPE=SUBMIT VALUE="Send comments">
```

A submit button can also have a NAME attribute, although this is rarely used. You will see later in this lesson how this affects the values sent to PHP.

The <TEXTAREA> Tag

The <TEXTAREA> tag is used to create a multiple-line text input item. In many respects, it behaves just like a TEXT type input tag, but the way it is formed in HTML is slightly different.

Because the initial value in a text area could span many lines, it is not given in a VALUE attribute. Instead, the starting value appears between a pair of tags, as follows:

```
<TEXTAREA ROWS=4 COLS=50 NAME="comments">
Enter your comments here
</TEXTAREA>
```

PHP is not concerned with what type of input a value comes from; the difference between a text area and text input is an HTML issue only.

The <SELECT> Tag

The final form item we will look at is the <SELECT> item, correctly known as a *menu* but more commonly called a *drop-down list*.

The most common use of a menu is to prompt for a single selection from a predefined list of values. The following example builds a drop-down list of possible places that visitors may have heard about your website:

```
<SELECT NAME="referrer">
<OPTION VALUE="search">Internet Search Engine</OPTION>
<OPTION VALUE="tv">TV Advertisement</OPTION>
<OPTION VALUE="billboard">Billboard</OPTION>
<OPTION SELECTED VALUE="other">Other</OPTION>
</SELECT>
```

In this case, the SELECTED attribute makes "Other" the default selection, even though it appears at the top of the list. If no item has the SELECTED attribute, the first option in the list is selected by default.

Putting It All Together

By putting all these form elements together and adding some label text and a little formatting, you can create a simple comments submission form that you can then process in PHP, as shown in Listing 11.1.

LISTING 11.1 A Web Form for Submitting User Comments

```
<FORM ACTION="send_comments.php" METHOD=POST>
<TABLE>
<TR>
  <TD>Your name:</TD>
  <TD><INPUT TYPE="TEXT" NAME="name" SIZE=30></TD>
</TR>
<TR>
  <TD>Your email:</TD>
  <TD><INPUT TYPE="TEXT" NAME="email" SIZE=30></TD>
</TR>
<TR>
  <TD>Your gender:</TD>
  <TD><INPUT TYPE="RADIO" NAME="gender" VALUE="m"> Male
      <INPUT TYPE="RADIO" NAME="gender" VALUE="f"> Female
  </TD>
</TR>
<TR>
  <TD>How you found us</TD>
  <TD>
    <SELECT NAME="referrer">
    <OPTION VALUE="search">Internet Search Engine</OPTION>
    <OPTION VALUE="tv">TV Advertisement</OPTION>
    <OPTION VALUE="billboard">Billboard</OPTION>
    <OPTION SELECTED VALUE="other">Other</OPTION>
    </SELECT>
  </TD>
</TR>
<TR>
  <TD>May we email you?</TD>
  <TD><INPUT TYPE="CHECKBOX" NAME="may_contact"
```

continues

LISTING 11.1   Continued

```
                 VALUE="Y" CHECKED></TD>
</TR>
<TR>
  <TD>Comments</TD>
  <TD><TEXTAREA ROWS=4 COLS=50
      NAME="comments">Enter your comments here
      </TEXTAREA></TD>
</TR>

</TABLE>

<INPUT TYPE="SUBMIT" VALUE="Send comments">
</FORM>
```

Processing a Form with PHP

Now let's look at how each type of item in a form is handled by PHP after the submit button is clicked.

Accessing Form Values

Form values are made available in PHP by using some special array structures. The arrays $_GET and $_POST contain values submitted using the GET and POST methods, respectively. A hybrid array, $_REQUEST, contains the contents of both of these arrays, as well as the values from $_COOKIE, which you will use in Lesson 14, "Cookies and Sessions."

> ✎ **Super-globals** The system-generated arrays that have names beginning with an underscore character are known as *super-globals* because they can be referenced from anywhere in a PHP script, regardless of scope. For instance, you do not need to explicitly declare $_POST as global to access its elements within a function.

Accessing the values from form items is fairly intuitive: The form item names become the element keys in $_GET or $_POST, and each value in the array is the value of the corresponding element when it was submitted.

For example, the email address submitted by comments.html will be $_POST["email"], and the comments text will be $_POST["comments"].

For CHECKBOX and RADIO input types, the VALUE attribute determines the value seen by PHP. If the check box named may_contact is checked, then the array element $_POST["may_contact"] has the value Y. If it is not checked, this element simply does not exist in the array; you should use isset to check whether a check box is checked.

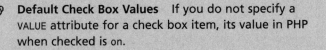

Default Check Box Values If you do not specify a VALUE attribute for a check box item, its value in PHP when checked is on.

The radio group gender causes $_POST["gender"] to contain the value m or f, depending on which value is selected and, as with a check box, if no value is selected, the array element does not exist.

The simplest way to see all the submitted data from a form is to use a call to print_r to dump out the contents of $_POST, as follows:

```
echo "<PRE>";
print_r($_POST);
echo "</PRE>";
```

This is a useful debugging technique if you want to see exactly what data is being passed to a script from a form. If you create send_comments.php, containing just these lines, the output shows you the value of each form element in turn. The following is sample output:

```
Array
(
    [name] => Chris Newman
    [email] => chris@lightwood.net
    [gender] => m
```

```
[referrer] => search
[may_contact] => Y
[comments] => This is my favorite website ever
)
```

Even the value of a submit button can be seen by PHP if the button is given a name and the button is clicked when the form is submitted. The following form has two buttons with different names, so that you can use PHP to determine which button was actually clicked:

```
<FORM ACTION="button.php" METHOD=POST>
<INPUT TYPE="SUBMIT" NAME="button1" VALUE="Button 1">
<INPUT TYPE="SUBMIT" NAME="button2" VALUE="Button 2">
</FORM>
```

In button.php, you could use a condition similar to the following to see which button is clicked:

```
if (isset($_POST["button1"])) {
  echo "You clicked button 1";
}
elseif (isset($_POST["button2"])) {
  echo "You clicked button 2";
}
else {
  echo "I don't know which button you clicked!";
}
```

The VALUE attribute of a submit button determines what label appears on the button itself, but that value is also the value that is passed to PHP when the button is clicked.

Submit Buttons   Many modern web browsers submit a form when you press the Enter key when focused on any of the input fields. Even if there is only one submit button on a form, its value is not sent to PHP unless it is actually clicked with the mouse.

Hidden Inputs

One other type of form input is available, and it can be used to pass values between scripts without their being visible on the web page itself.

The HIDDEN type takes NAME and VALUE attributes, as usual, but it simply acts a placeholder for that value.

The following hidden input is passed to the PHP script when the form is submitted, and $_POST["secret"] contains the value from the form:

```
<INPUT TYPE="HIDDEN" NAME="secret" VALUE="this is a secret">
```

Be aware, however, that HIDDEN attribute inputs are not secure for transmitting passwords and other sensitive data. Although they do not appear on the web page, if you view the page source, you can still see hidden values in the HTML code.

Creating a Form Mail Script

The desired result from the comments form you've been working with in this lesson is to provide a way of sending user-submitted comments by email to the owner of a website. Now you'll learn how to put together a form handler script to create this component for a website.

The mail Function

PHP's mail function sends an email message, using your system's mailer program. On Linux/Unix systems, the sendmail utility is used to put a message into the outbound queue. On Windows machines, it usually sends via SMTP, and the name of the relay server must be defined in php.ini for this to work properly. Lesson 20, "PHP Configuration," looks at configuration issues in more detail.

The three required arguments to mail are the recipient's email address, the message subject, and the message body. An optional fourth argument can contain additional mail headers to be sent; this is useful for setting the From: address or adding a Cc: recipient.

The script send_comments.php in Listing 11.2 takes the data sent from the comments form and sends it on to the owner of the website by email.

This script performs a loop through all the elements in $_POST and builds up the string $body, which becomes the body text of the email message. Note that \n characters are used to separate lines in the output because a plain-text email is created, which means no HTML formatting is required.

LISTING 11.2   send_comments.php

```php
<?php

$body = "These comments were sent via the website\n\n";

foreach($_POST as $field => $value) {
  $body .= sprintf("%s = %s\n", $field, $value);
}

mail("owner@website.com", "Comments sent via website", $body,
          'From: "WebComments" <comments@website.com>');

?>
<H1>Thank You</H1>
Your comments have been sent!
```

The email sent to the site owner should look something like the following:

```
The following comments were submitted via the website

name = Chris Newman
email = chris@lightwood.net
gender = m
referrer = search
may_contact = Y
comments = This is my favorite website ever
```

The format of this email is very rough because each line is generated automatically. Of course, if you prefer, you could spend much longer creating a nicely formatted email; for instance, you could replace the coded values of gender and referrer with their full descriptions.

Summary

In this lesson you have learned how to process user-submitted data from HTML forms. In the next lesson you will learn how to use PHP to create HTML form items such as menus and radio button groups on-the-fly.

LESSON 12

Generating Dynamic HTML

In this lesson you will learn how to create elements of an HTML form by using PHP. These techniques enable you to specify default values for input items and create dynamic drop-down menus or radio button groups based on data in a script.

Setting Default Values

Let's begin with some simple examples that embed PHP within form elements to set the default values of some items when the page is loaded.

Default Input Values

The default value of a text input is given in the VALUE attribute. This value displays in the field when the page is loaded, and, unless it is overtyped, the same value is sent to the PHP processing script when the form is submitted.

Consider a shopping cart page for an online store, where customers are given the opportunity to change the quantity of each item in their cart before finalizing the order. The current quantity of each line item would be displayed in a small text input box and could be overtyped, and then the user would be able to click a button to refresh the contents of the cart. Listing 12.1 is a very simple example of this, for a store that sells only one product but allows you to choose the quantity to buy.

LISTING 12.1   Defaulting the Value of a Text Input Field

```php
<?php
if(isset($_POST["quantity"]))
  $quantity = settype($_POST["quantity"], "integer");
else
  $quantity = 1;

$item_price = 5.99;
printf("%d x item = $%.2f",
        $quantity, $quantity * $item_price);
?>
<FORM ACTION="buy.php" METHOD=POST>
Update quantity:
<INPUT NAME="quantity" SIZE=2
 VALUE="<?php echo $quantity;?>">
<INPUT TYPE=SUBMIT VALUE="Change quantity">
</FORM>
```

First of all, you set an overall default value for $quantity of 1, so that the first time the page is loaded, this is the quantity displayed in the field and used to calculate the total price. Then, inside the VALUE tag, you run a single PHP statement to echo the value of $quantity. If a quantity value is posted to the form, then that value is used instead.

This script should be called buy.php so that the form posts to itself when submitted. If you change the quantity value and press the submit button, the script calculates the new total price. Also, the quantity input field defaults to the value you just entered when the page reloads.

Checking a Check Box

The CHECKED attribute determines whether a check box is on or off by default when a page loads. Using PHP, you can embed a condition within the <INPUT> tag to determine whether to include the CHECKED attribute on a check box:

```php
<INPUT TYPE="CHECKBOX"
 NAME="mybox" <?php if(condition) echo "CHECKED";?>>
```

The way this looks can be confusing, particularly because two > symbols appear at the end of the tag—one to close the PHP section and one to close the <INPUT> tag. In fact, the position of the CHECKED attribute is not important, so depending on your preference, you can move it around for readability:

```
<INPUT <?php if(condition) echo "CHECKED";?>
 TYPE="CHECKBOX" NAME="mybox">
```

> **Closing PHP Tags** When embedding small chunks of PHP, you should always try to include the closing ?> tag as soon as possible. If you miss this closing tag, PHP attempts to interpret the subsequent HTML as PHP and is likely to come up with some interesting error messages!

Spacing can be very important when you're using PHP within HTML. In the previous example, if there is not a space on either side of the PHP statement and the condition is true, the actual HTML produced is as follows:

```
<INPUT CHECKEDTYPE="CHECKBOX" NAME="mybox">
```

Because CHECKEDTYPE is not recognized as part of the <INPUT> tag, your browser is likely to display this as a text input box, not a check box! It's always better to have too much space around dynamic elements in HTML tags than to risk not having enough.

Selecting a Radio Button Group Item

The CHECKED attribute is also used to specify which item in a radio button group should be selected by default. For example, an online store may offer three shipping options, with each having a different cost. To make sure the customer always chooses a shipping option, one of the selections would be picked by default, with the option to change it if desired (a radio button cannot be deselected except when another button in the same group is selected):

```
<INPUT TYPE="RADIO" CHECKED
 NAME="shipping" VALUE="economy"> Economy
<INPUT TYPE="RADIO" NAME="shipping" VALUE="express"> Standard
<INPUT TYPE="RADIO" NAME="shipping" VALUE="express"> Express
```

To dynamically assign the CHECKED attribute to one of the items in the
radio button group, each one must contain a condition that checks the current value of $shipping against the value that corresponds to that item.
Listing 12.2 gives an example.

LISTING 12.2   Selecting a Default Radio Button Group Item

```php
<?php
if (!isset($shipping))
  $shipping = "economy";

echo "Your order will be sent via $shipping shipping";
?>
<FORM ACTION="shipping.php" METHOD=POST>


<INPUT TYPE="RADIO" NAME="shipping" VALUE="economy"
 <?php if ($shipping == "economy") echo "CHECKED";?>> Economy


<INPUT TYPE="RADIO" NAME="shipping" VALUE="standard"
 <?php if ($shipping == "standard") echo "CHECKED";?>>
   Standard


<INPUT TYPE="RADIO" NAME="shipping" VALUE="express"
 <?php if ($shipping == "express") echo "CHECKED";?>> Express
<INPUT TYPE="SUBMIT" VALUE="Change shipping option">
</FORM>
```

Notice how cumbersome this is, even for a short radio button group of
just three items. Later in this lesson you will learn how to create radio
button groups on-the-fly so that larger radio button groups can be man-
aged in a much more elegant way.

Defaulting a Selection in a Menu

The SELECTED attribute in an <OPTION> tag specifies which item is to be
selected by default. If no item has the SELECTED attribute, the first item in
the list is shown by default.

Using PHP to display the SELECTED attribute against the appropriate
option is just as cumbersome as picking the selected item in a radio button

group, and the same technique applies. Listing 12.3 shown the same example of shipping rates as in Listing 12.2, using a drop-down menu instead of a radio button group.

LISTING 12.3   Selecting a Default Item from a Menu

```
<?php
if (!isset($shipping))
  $shipping = "economy";

echo "Your order will be sent via $shipping shipping";
?>
<FORM ACTION="shipping.php" METHOD=POST>
<SELECT NAME="shipping">
<OPTION <?php if ($shipping == "economy") echo "SELECTED";?>
   VALUE="economy">Economy</OPTION>
<OPTION <?php if ($shipping == "standard") echo "SELECTED";?>
   VALUE="standard">Standard</OPTION>
<OPTION <?php if ($shipping == "express") echo "SELECTED";?>
   VALUE="express">Express</OPTION>
<INPUT TYPE="SUBMIT" VALUE="Change shipping option">
</FORM>
```

As with a radio button group, using a function to generate on-the-fly menus allows you to work with much larger option lists and still dynamically select a chosen option.

Creating Form Elements

Now let's look at how some of the items in an HTML form can be generated by using custom PHP functions. This type of modularization means that you can use a function over and over again whenever you need to include the same type of item on a form.

Creating a Dynamic Radio Button Group

A modular routine to generate a radio button group requires three pieces of information: the name of the group, a list of values, and a list of labels. You can use an associative array to pass the values and labels to the function in one go.

Say you want to be able to generate the HTML for a radio button group
by using simple code similar to the following:

```
$options = array("economy"  => "Economy",
                 "standard" => "Standard",
                 "express"  => "Express");
$default = "economy";
$html = generate_radio_group("shipping", $options, $default);
```

As you can see, this is the kind of function you are likely to use again and
again when creating HTML forms, and it is very useful to build up a tool-
box of similar functions to make it easy to perform common tasks. Here's
how the generate_radio_group function might be implemented:

```
function generate_radio_group($name, $options, $default="") {
  $name = htmlentities($name);
  foreach($options as $value => $label) {
    $value = htmlentities($value);
    $html .= "<INPUT TYPE=\"RADIO\" ";
    if ($value == $default)
      $html .= "CHECKED ";
    $html .= "NAME=\"$name\" VALUE=\"$value\">";
    $html .= $label . "<br>";
  }
  return($html);
}
```

At the heart of the function is a loop through $options that generates
each <INPUT> tag in turn, giving each tag the same NAME attribute but a
different VALUE attribute. The label text is placed next to each button, and
in this sample function, the only formatting is to place a <br> tag between
each button in the group. You could format the options in a table or in any
other way you see fit.

At each step of the loop, the script compares the current value of $value
with the passed-in $default value. If they match, the CHECKED attribute is
included in the generated HTML. Again, spacing is important here; note
that the space after CHECKED is added to the HTML string.

The $default argument is specified as optional. If generate_
radio_group is called with only two arguments, none of the radio buttons
will be selected by default.

> **HTML Entities**   The htmlentities function is used to replace certain characters in a string with corresponding HTML entities. Because the values of $name and $value are output inside another HTML tag, the htmlentities function is important to ensure that there are no characters in those strings that could break the tag.

Creating a Dynamic Menu

The process for creating a drop-down menu is very similar to that for creating a radio button group. Again, a loop is required—this time to generate an <OPTION> tag for each option in turn. The function also needs to include the <SELECT> and </SELECT> tags around the option list. The function generate_menu would look like this:

```
function generate_menu($name, $options, $default="") {

  $html = "<SELECT NAME=\"$name\">";
  foreach($options as $value => $label) {
    $html .= "<OPTION ";
    if ($value == $default)
      $html .= "SELECTED ";
    $html .= "VALUE=\"$value\">$label</OPTION>";
  }
  $html .= "</SELECT>";
  return($html);
}
```

The string returned by this function contains the entire HTML code to produce a drop-down menu that contains the supplied options. You might prefer to have the function return only the option tags and place your own <SELECT> tags around them; this would allow you to easily add a JavaScript onChange event on the menu, for instance.

Multiple Selection Items

When used with the MULTIPLE attribute, the <SELECT> form item allows a user to choose multiple options from a menu, usually by holding the Ctrl key while clicking the options. To handle more than one selection in PHP, the input name must be an array. Then when the form is posted, the elements in the array contain the values of each selected item in turn.

For example, if you create a multiple-selection menu by using the following HTML and submit it to a PHP script that contains just a `print_r` instruction, you see that `$_POST["colors"]` is an array that contains one element for each option selected:

```
<SELECT MULTIPLE NAME="colors[]">
<OPTION VALUE="red">Red</OPTION>
<OPTION VALUE="white">White</OPTION>
<OPTION VALUE="blue">Blue</OPTION>
</SELECT>
```

With all three of the options selected, `$_POST["colors"]` contains three elements with numeric indices 0 to 2, having values red, white, and blue, respectively.

The same principle applies to any type of form input. If more than one item exists with the same name but the name ends with a pair of square brackets, an array is created in PHP with that name, containing elements for each of those items' values.

This is most useful when you're implementing a multiple-selection input using check boxes. Rather than having to give each check box a unique name, you can give each the name of an array. The array created when the form is submitted contains an element for each item checked.

The final example in this lesson involves the function generate_checkboxes, which creates a set of check boxes with the same name that can be used as an alternative to <SELECT MULTIPLE> to implement a multiple-option selection in an HTML form. The function, along with a simple example of its usage, is shown in Listing 12.4

LISTING 12.4   Creating a Multiple-Option Selection Using Check Boxes

```php
<?php

function generate_checkboxes($name,
                $options, $default=array()) {
```

```php
  if (!is_array($default))
    $default = array();

  foreach($options as $value => $label) {
    $html .= "<INPUT TYPE=CHECKBOX ";
    if (in_array($value, $default))
      $html .= "CHECKED ";
    $html .= "NAME=\"{$name}[]\" VALUE=\"$value\">";
    $html .= $label . "<br>";
  }
  return($html);
}

$options = array("movies" => "Going to the movies",
                 "music"  => "Listening to music",
                 "sport"  => "Playing or watching sports",
                 "travel" => "Traveling");

$html = generate_checkboxes("interests",
                                $options, $interests);

?>
<H1>Please select your interests</H1>
<FORM ACTION="interests.php" METHOD=POST>
<?php print $html;?>
<INPUT TYPE=SUBMIT VALUE="Continue">
</FORM>
```

In the function generate_checkboxes, the $default argument is an array rather than a single value; after all, more than one of the options might be selected by default. The array passed in as $default can be exactly the same array that is submitted to PHP by the HTML that this function creates.

To find out whether each check box should have the CHECKED attribute, in_array is called to see whether the current option name is in the list of default values. If $value appears anywhere in $default, the check box will be checked when the page loads.

Listing 12.4 shows this function in action, using a section of a web page that asks a user about her interests. She can select any number of items from the list, and, in this example, the script submits to itself with the options remaining checked so that the user can change her mind if she wants to.

In the array $interests created in PHP, each element is a key name from $options. If you want to find the label that corresponds to each selected option, you can reference the corresponding element from $options.

Summary

In this lesson you have learned how to generate HTML components on-the-fly and learned some techniques for creating dynamic form input objects. In the next lesson you will learn how to perform validation on an HTML form.

LESSON 13

Form Validation

In this lesson you will learn some techniques for validating form input in a user-friendly way.

The principles of validating user-submitted input are fairly straightforward: Just check each item in $_POST in turn and make sure it matches a set of criteria. However, making sure the user is able to correct any mistakes and resubmit the form with a minimum of fuss presents a bit more of a challenge.

Enforcing Required Fields

The most basic type of form validation is to enforce that a particular field must contain a value. In the case of a text input that is submitted with no value entered, the element in $_POST is still created, but it contains an empty value. Therefore, you cannot use isset to check whether a value was entered; you must check the actual value of the element, either by comparing it to an empty string or by using the following, more compact syntax with the Boolean NOT operator:

```
if (!$_POST["fieldname"]) { ... }
```

Because each field on the form creates an element in $_POST, if every field requires a value to be entered, you could use a simple loop to check that there are no empty values in the array:

```
foreach($_POST as $field => $value) {
  if (!$value) {
    $err .= "$field is a required field <br>";
  }
}
if ($err) {
```

```
    echo $err;
    echo "Press the back button to fix these errors";
}
else {
    // Continue with script
}
```

Rather than exit as soon as an empty field is found, this script builds up an error string, $err. After the validation is done, the contents of $err are displayed if there are any errors. If there are no errors, $err is empty, and script execution continues with the else clause.

Validation Warnings   Always show all the warning messages that relate to the submitted data straight away. You should give your users the opportunity to correct their errors all at one time.

One obvious limitation of this approach is that you cannot pick which fields require a value; every posted field must have been completed. You could improve upon this by supplying a list of required fields in the script, and by using an associative array, you can also provide a label for each field to display in the warning message:

```
$required = array("first_name" => "First name",
                  "email"      => "Email address",
                  "telephone"  => "Telephone number");
foreach($required as $field => $label) {
    if (!$_POST[$field]) {
        $err .= "$label is a required field <br>";
    }
}
```

Displaying Validation Warnings

Another issue to consider is where to send the user when validation fails. So far we have assumed that a form submits to a processing script, and when one or more validation errors are found, the form prompts the user to use his or her browser's Back button to fix the errors.

Not only does this create one more step for the user to take in order to complete the form—and in an online store, you want as few obstacles between a customer and a completed order as possible—it can also sometimes cause the data in the form fields to be lost when Back is clicked.

Whether the Back button causes data to be lost usually depends on the cache settings, either on the web server, in the user's browser, or at the user's Internet service provider. In many cases there is no problem. However, most notably when a PHP session has been started, no-cache headers are automatically sent to the browser, which causes data in form fields to be reset to their original values when you click the Back button. You will learn more about PHP sessions in Lesson 14, "Cookies and Sessions."

A good technique is to have the form and processing script in the same file and have the form submit to itself. This way, if there are errors, they can be displayed on the same page as the form itself, and the previously entered values can be automatically defaulted into the form.

Listing 13.1 shows a fairly complete example of a registration form, register.php. The name and email address fields are required, but the telephone number is optional.

LISTING 13.1   A Sample Registration Form with Required Fields

```php
<?php

$required = array("name"  => "Your Name",
                  "email" => "Email Address");

foreach($required as $field => $label) {
  if (!$_POST[$field]) {
    $err .= "$label is a required field <br>";
  }
}

if ($err) {
  echo $err;

?>
<FORM ACTION="register.php" METHOD=POST>
```

LISTING 13.1   Continued

```
<TABLE BORDER=0>
<TR>
  <TD>Your Name</TD>
  <TD><INPUT TYPE=TEXT SIZE=30 NAME="name"
              VALUE="<?php echo $_POST["name"];?>"></TD>
</TR>
<TR>
  <TD>Email Address</TD>
  <TD><INPUT TYPE=TEXT SIZE=30 NAME="email"
              VALUE="<?php echo $_POST["email"];?>"></TD>
</TR>
<TR>
  <TD>Telephone</TD>
  <TD><INPUT TYPE=TEXT SIZE=12 NAME="telephone"
              VALUE="<?php echo $_POST["telephone"];?>"></TD>
</TR>
</TABLE>
<INPUT TYPE=SUBMIT VALUE="Register">
</FORM>

<?php
}
else {
  echo "Thank you for registering";
}
?>
```

Note that the warning messages in this example appears even if the form
has not yet been submitted. This could be improved by also checking for
the existence of the $_POST array in the script by using is_array, but the
check for $err would also need to look for $_POST; otherwise, the form
would never be displayed.

The condition that checks $err spans the HTML form and, even though
the PHP tags are closed around this chunk of HTML, the form is displayed only if that condition is true.

In this example, after the form has been completed successfully, only a
simple message is displayed. This is where you would do any processing
based on the submitted data, such as storing it to a database, which you
will learn about in Lesson 19, "Using a MySQL Database." Alternatively,

the script could force the browser to redirect the user to another page automatically by using a `Location` HTTP header, as follows:

```
header("Location: newpage.php");
```

Enforcing Data Rules

You will often want to ensure not only that data is entered into required fields but that the quality of the data is good enough before proceeding. For instance, you might want to check that an email address or a phone number has the right format, using the rules developed in Lesson 8, "Regular Expressions." You could also enforce a minimum length on a field to make sure a user cannot just enter an x in each field to continue to the next page.

Because each field will probably have a different validation rule, you cannot enforce data rules in a loop; you must instead write a rule for each field to be checked. However, when used in conjunction with the check for empty fields in a loop from the previous examples, you should also check that the value has been entered before doing any further validation. Otherwise, the warning message will first tell a user that a field is required and then also that it has been entered in the wrong format!

The following rules could be added to Listing 13.1 after the required fields check to enforce suitable values for email address and telephone number:

```
if ($_POST["email"] &&
   !ereg("^[^@]+@([a-z0-9\-]+\.)+[a-z]{2,4}$",
       $_POST["email"]))
   $err .= "Email address format was incorrect <br>";

if ($_POST["telephone"] &&
   !ereg("^\(([[:digit:]]{3}\)[[:digit:]]{3}-[[:digit:]]{4}$",
       $_POST["telephone"]))
   $err .= "Telephone must be in format (555)555-5555 <br>";
```

Because these additional rules add new messages to $err if an error is found, the rest of the script remains unchanged.

Highlighting Fields That Require Attention

Rather than bombard the user with a list of warning messages, it's more user-friendly to highlight the fields in the form that require attention.

The technique to use here is very similar to the previous example, but rather than append each warning message to $err, you should give each field its own warning text. If you use an array of warnings, it's simple to see whether the form has been successfully validated by counting the elements in $warnings.

You write each rule to add an element to $warnings if validation of that field fails, as shown in the following example:

```
if (!ereg("^[^@]+@([a-z\-]+\.)+[a-z]{2,4}$",
        $_POST["email"]))
    $warnings["email"] = "Invalid Format";
```

Then in the form itself, you can display this warning text next to the corresponding field:

```
<TR>
  <TD>Email Address</TD>
  <TD><INPUT TYPE=TEXT SIZE=30 NAME="email"
            VALUE="<?php echo $_POST["email"];?>"></TD>
  <TD><b><?php echo $warnings["email"];?></b></TD>
</TR>
```

Listing 13.2 shows a revised register.php file that uses this technique to highlight missing or invalid field values.

LISTING 13.2   Form Validation Using Inline Warnings

```
<?php

$required = array("name"  => "Your Name",
                  "email" => "Email Address");

foreach($required as $field => $label) {
  if (!$_POST[$field]) {
    $warnings[$field] = "Required";
```

```
  }
}

if ($_POST["email"] &&
    !ereg("^[^@]+@([a-z\-]+\.)+[a-z]{2,4}$", $_POST["email"]))
  $warnings["email"] = "Invalid email";

if ($_POST["telephone"] &&
    !ereg("^\([[:digit:]]{3}\)[[:digit:]]{3}-[[:digit:]]{4}$",
        $_POST["telephone"]))
  $warnings["telephone"] = "Must be (555)555-5555";

if (count($warnings) > 0) {

?>
<FORM ACTION="register.php" METHOD=POST>
<TABLE BORDER=0>
<TR>
  <TD>Your Name</TD>
  <TD><INPUT TYPE=TEXT SIZE=30 NAME="name"
             VALUE="<?php echo $_POST["name"];?>"></TD>
  <TD><?php echo $warnings["name"];?></TD>
</TR>
<TR>
  <TD>Email Address</TD>
  <TD><INPUT TYPE=TEXT SIZE=30 NAME="email"
             VALUE="<?php echo $_POST["email"];?>"></TD>
  <TD><?php echo $warnings["email"];?></TD>
</TR>
<TR>
  <TD>Telephone</TD>
  <TD><INPUT TYPE=TEXT SIZE=12 NAME="telephone"
             VALUE="<?php echo $_POST["telephone"];?>"></TD>
  <TD><?php echo $warnings["telephone"];?></TD>
</TR>
</TABLE>
<INPUT TYPE=SUBMIT VALUE="Register">
</FORM>

<?php
}
else {
  echo "Thank you for registering";
}
?>
```

The first loop assigns the warning text "Required" to any required field that is left blank. Each of the individual validation rules has its own warning text.

How you highlight a field that requires attention is up to your imagination and creativity with HTML. For instance, by checking for the presence of an element in $warnings for each field, you could change the style of the input box to a shaded background, like so:

```
<INPUT TYPE=TEXT SIZE=30 NAME="email"
<?php if ($warnings["email"]) echo "STYLE=\"shaded\"";?>
VALUE="<?php echo $_POST["email"];?>">
```

Summary

In this lesson you have learned how to validate user input from HTML forms and how to present the form back to the user so that he or she can correct any errors. In the next lesson you will learn about cookies and sessions in PHP.

LESSON 14
Cookies and Sessions

This lesson examines two ways of passing data between pages of a website without requiring a form submission from one page to another: using cookies and using sessions.

Cookies

Cookies are small pieces of information that are stored in your web browser. They typically contain data that is used to identify you when you look at a website so that site can be customized for each visitor.

Rather than having to pass data to a script by using a form or as values in the query string, cookies are sent back to your scripts automatically by your web browser. Even if you go off and browse to another website, their values are remembered when you return.

For example, if you have to log in to access a particular website, you may be able to let a cookie remember your username so you do not have to type it each time you go back. In this case, you only have to enter your password. Or on a community site, your browser might record the date you last visited in a cookie, so that any forum messages posted since you last visited can be highlighted as new.

Cookie Ingredients

Each cookie consists of a name and a value, just like regular variables in PHP. The instruction to create a cookie in your web browser is sent as an HTTP header before a web page is transmitted; when your web browser sees this header, it takes the appropriate action.

The HTTP headers that create cookies are the same, regardless of whether they are generated by PHP or any other means of interfacing with your web server. The header used to set a cookie called `email` might look like this:

```
Set-Cookie: email=chris@lightwood.net
```

> 🖉 **HTTP Headers**   You will never see an actual HTTP header in your web browser. We will look at how different types of HTTP headers are sent in PHP in Lesson 16, "Communicating with the Web Server."

A cookie also has an expiration date; some cookies last only as long as your web browser is open and are kept in your computer's memory, whereas others have a fixed expiration date in the future and are saved to your hard disk. The HTTP header to set the email cookie that will expire at the end of 2005 would look like this:

```
Set-Cookie: email=chris@lightwood.net;
            expires=Sat, 31-Dec-2005 23:59:59 GMT
```

If no `expires` attribute is sent in the `Set-Cookie` header, the cookie will be destroyed when the web browser is closed.

The other attributes that can be set are the domain name and the path by which a browser will send back a cookie. When you make any subsequent visit to a page for which you have a cookie set, its name and value are sent to the web server.

The default behavior is to send a cookie back to any page on the same domain that it was set from. By setting the domain and path, you can tell the cookie to be sent back to other subdomains or only to scripts in a certain part of the site.

The following header creates an email cookie that is sent back to any subdomain of lightwood.net, as long as the page requested is in the /scripts subdirectory:

```
Set-Cookie: email=chris@lightwood.net; domain=.lightwood.net;
            path=/scripts
```

> **Subdomains** You can only set the `domain` attribute of a cookie to a variant of the domain from which the cookie was originally set, or to `.yourdomain.com` to indicate all subdomains.
>
> This is a security measure to prevent some websites from being able to confuse others. For example, you cannot set a cookie that would be sent back to www.php.net from any website that is not hosted at php.net.

Accessing Cookies

The `$_COOKIE` super-global array in PHP contains all the cookies that have been sent to the current script. Cookies are sent back to the web server in an HTTP header, and PHP builds the `$_COOKIE` array based on this information.

You can access cookies in the same way that you reference posted form data. For example, the following statement displays the current value of the email cookie:

```
echo $_COOKIE["email"];
```

If you ever feel that your cookies are getting in a bit of a mess, you can just create a script to dump them all out to screen so you can see what's going on. It is as simple as this:

```
echo "<PRE>";
print_r($_COOKIES);
echo "</PRE>";
```

Making Cookies with PHP

Although you have now seen how to create cookies by using HTTP headers, you will probably not use this method again because PHP contains a function that makes cookie setting much easier:

```
setcookie("email", "chris@lightwood.net", time() + 3600);
```

Rather than the strictly formatted textual date shown in the header example earlier in this lesson, you specify the expiration date in `setcookie` as a Unix timestamp. This makes it easy to set a cookie that lasts for a fixed amount of time or until a date and time in the future.

> **Expiration Times**   The expiration argument specifies the latest date and time that a stored cookie will be transmitted. As time comparison is performed on the local computer, the actual expiration of cookies is determined by the local system clock and, if that clock is incorrect, is beyond your control.

The next two optional arguments are used to specify the domain and path for the cookie. If you want to set a domain and path but not an expiration time, you use NULL for the third argument:

```
setcookie("email", "chris@lightwood.net", NULL,
          ".lightwood.net", "/scripts");
```

The final optional argument to `setcookie` is a flag that tells the browser to send the cookie back to the server only over an SSL encrypted connection—in other words, only for web pages with addresses that begin https://.

> **Password Cookies**   As handy as it may be to have a password stored in a cookie so that you can be automatically logged in to a website when you revisit it, this is very dangerous, even when the secure flag is set.
>
> Cookies are stored in plain text and can be viewed simply by looking in the correct place on your hard disk. Malicious spyware programs exist that try to steal your passwords by searching through your cookies!

Deleting Cookies

There is no `unsetcookie` function to tell the web browser to delete a cookie. To stop a cookie value from being sent back to the web server, you use `setcookie` with an empty value and an expiration date that has already passed.

The following example unsets the email cookie by using an expiration value that is one hour ago:

```
setcookie("email", "", time() - 3600);
```

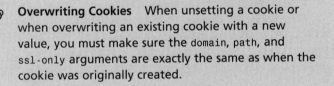

Overwriting Cookies   When unsetting a cookie or when overwriting an existing cookie with a new value, you must make sure the `domain`, `path`, and `ssl-only` arguments are exactly the same as when the cookie was originally created.

Sessions

Sessions are very similar to cookies in that they can be used for passing values between pages of a website. Rather than storing the values in each web browser, however, the values are stored on the web server, and a single identity cookie is used to tell PHP which set of values corresponds to the current user.

Because much less data is sent back and forth between the web server and browser, sessions are more efficient than cookies when larger amounts of data are stored.

Creating a Session

To initialize a new session in a PHP script, you use the `session_start` function. You can use an optional argument to specify a session name, but usually this is not required. Every script on your site that starts the same session will be able to access the same set of session variables.

The call to `session_start` to create a new session is as simple as the following:

```
session_start();
```

The `$_SESSION` super-global array is used to store and retrieve session variables. Unlike the other super-globals you have encountered so far, you can assign values directly to `$_SESSION`, after which they are available to any script that shares the session.

Consider the script in Listing 14.1, which maintains two session variables—a count of the number of times you have viewed the page and the timestamp of the last visit.

LISTING 14.1   Using Session Variables to Track Visits to a Page

```php
<?php

session_start();

if ($_SESSION["last_visit"]) {
  echo "Date of last visit: ";
  echo date("j F Y, H:i:s", $_SESSION["last_visit"]);
  echo "<br>";
  echo "Total visits: ".$_SESSION["num_visits"];
}
else
  echo "This is your first visit";

$_SESSION["last_visit"] = time();
$_SESSION["num_visits"]++;
?>
```

Each time the page is loaded, the old values are displayed and the new values set. Notice that if you surf to other websites and then come back, these values are remembered, but if you close your web browser and come back, the values are reset.

Using Session Variables

One of the advantages of session variables over cookies is their ability to use PHP's data types. Cookie values are always simple text values, but a session variable can take any value that a regular PHP variable can.

For instance, to store a list of items in a cookie, you would have to create an array and pass it to serialize to store. By using a session variable, you can create an array directly and store that data structure in the session.

The example in Listing 14.2 uses an array stored in the session to retain a list of values entered through a form. This is a fairly trivial example, but it demonstrates the flexibility you have when using session variables.

LISTING 14.2   Using Arrays as Session Variables

```php
<?php

session_start();

if (isset($_POST["word"]))
  $_SESSION["words"][] = $_POST["word"];

if (is_array($_SESSION["words"])) {
  foreach($_SESSION["words"] as $word) {
    echo $word . "<br>";
  }
}

?>
<FORM ACTION="list.php" METHOD=POST>
Enter a word: <INPUT SIZE="10" NAME="word">
<INPUT TYPE=SUBMIT VALUE="Add word to list">
</FORM>
```

Summary

In this lesson you have learned how to set cookies from PHP and how to use PHP's session management to store values within a browser session. In the next lesson you will use these techniques to create a user authentication system using PHP.

LESSON 15

User Authentication

In this lesson you will build a user authentication process that can be used to protect certain pages of your website by using a password.

Types of Authentication

Chances are you have needed to log in to a website in the past, so you should be aware of how the process of authentication works from a user's point of view. Generally speaking, you are asked to enter a username— sometimes your email address—and a password.

There are actually two ways that a website can authenticate a user, though: using basic HTTP authentication and using session-based authentication. The following sections clarify the differences between these two methods.

Basic HTTP Authentication

Basic HTTP authentication can be performed by web server, without having anything to do with PHP script. The example in this section assumes that you are using Apache web server; for other web servers, you should refer to your documentation.

Authentication is usually done on a per-directory basis but can be set up to apply to individual files if required. By using an .htaccess file on your website, you can specify for that directory a custom configuration that instructs the web server to require a login before proceeding. A typical set of configuration directives would look like this:

```
AuthType Basic
AuthName "Protected Website"
```

```
AuthUserFile /home/yourname/htpasswd
require valid-user
```

`AuthUserFile` points to the location of a password file that is created by using the `htpasswd` program. To create a new password file, you would run a command like the following:

```
$ htpasswd -c /home/yourname/htpasswd chris
New password:
Re-type new password:
```

Password Files   You should use the `-c` switch only when you want to create a new file. The `htpasswd` program does not ask whether you want to overwrite an existing file. Running `htpasswd` without the `-c` option on an existing password file adds a user.

You have to enter the new password twice, after which an entry is added to the password file given. The entry consists of the username and an encrypted version of the password, separated with a colon character. However, you should never need to work with this file directly. A typical password file entry might look like this:

```
chris:XNiv7qSUTFPU6
damon:ZxxE2PTEXeVNU
shelley:SVzAEtxMLEAls
vanessa:cX/t1Pv2oQfrY
```

When you try to access a file in the protected directory, your web browser pops up a window that asks for a username and password, and the page requested loads only after you have entered the correct information.

The `require valid-user` directive instructs the web server to show the page to any authenticated user. You might want to grant access to only certain users, which you can do with the `require user` directive:

```
require user chris damon shelley
```

Basic HTTP authentication also allows you to set up user groups to give access to particular sections of the site only to certain users. You can then use the `require group` directive to specify access to one or more user groups.

The following groups file, usually named `htgroups`, divides the users in the password file into two groups:

```
boys: chris damon
girls: shelley vanessa
```

To give access only to the boys group, you could use the following `.htaccess` file:

```
AuthType Basic
AuthName "Boys Only"
AuthUserFile /home/yourname/htpasswd
AuthGroupFile /home/yourname/htgroup
require group boys
```

Although it is fairly easy to set up and reasonably flexible, basic HTTP authentication has some drawbacks. First, you cannot change the look and feel of the pop-up login box. If you want to customize the process at all, you cannot use this method. Furthermore, the password file is stored on the server's filesystem, and updating it from a script may be problematic; you will learn more about these issues when dealing with reading and writing to files in Lesson 17, "Filesystem Access."

> **Apache Add-ons**   Several third-party modules for the Apache web server—such as `mod_auth_mysql` and `mod_auth_sqlite`—allow you to use basic HTTP authentication with password information stored in a database. Check with your web host to see whether these modules are installed.

Session-Based Authentication

To provide a completely customizable login process for your website, you must implement it yourself, and doing so in PHP requires using session variables.

In a nutshell, once a user is logged in, the browser's session contains enough information to convince the scripts on the website that you are allowed to view a page. Users log in by using a form on your site where they enter their username and password. You can set up the layout and flow of the login process any way you see fit.

One fairly significant difference from basic HTTP authentication is that the instruction to check the validity of a user's session appears in the script itself, not in a per-directory configuration file.

Protecting HTML   If your website includes plain HTML files that contain no PHP, you need to add PHP code to them to prevent them from being viewable to an anonymous user. You also need to change their file extension to .php.

Building an Authentication System

The rest of this lesson walks you through building an authentication mechanism using PHP sessions.

How the System Works

There are two main components of the authentication system you're going to build now. First, you need a login processor that checks the validity of the username and password entered in the form. You also need a piece of code that can be put at the top of each script to check the session and make sure the user is authenticated before continuing.

Login Forms   You need to make sure you always use the POST method for login forms. Submitting a username and password by using the GET method causes these values to appear in the URL of the next page for anyone to see!

You should split off the session-checking code into an include file, auth.inc, so that it is simple to protect a page by simply putting the following statement at the top of the script:

```
include "auth.inc";
```

You can use a single session variable to store the username of the logged-in user. If the variable contains a username, that user is logged in; logging a user out is as simple as deleting this session variable. As long as nobody else shares the domain on which your website is hosted and could create a conflicting session, this is adequately secure. Knowing this, auth.inc can really be as simple as the following:

```
session_start();
if (!isset($_SESSION["auth_username"])) {
  echo "You must be logged in to view this page";
  exit;
}
```

Here you simply display a message and exit the script if the user is not logged in. You will see later on how you can improve this for usability, but you need to create the login process itself first.

Authenticating a Login

The login form, at its heart, needs to contain just two fields—username and password—and a submit button. As long as these are present, the form's layout is up to you. For now, you can keep it fairly plain, in a simple table layout. Listing 15.1 shown the basic login form.

LISTING 15.1   A Basic Login Form

```
<FORM ACTION="login.php" METHOD="POST">
<TABLE BORDER=0>
<TR>
  <TD>Username:</TD>
  <TD><INPUT TYPE="TEXT" SIZE=10 NAME="username"></TD>
</TR>
<TR>
  <TD>Password:</TD>
  <TD><INPUT TYPE="PASSWORD" SIZE=10 NAME="password"></TD>
</TR>
</TABLE>
```

```
<INPUT TYPE=SUBMIT VALUE="Log in">
</FORM>
```

 Password Fields   The PASSWORD type input works exactly the same way as a TEXT type, but the characters entered are obscured as they are typed. The only restriction on a password field is that it cannot be given a VALUE attribute for a default value.

The form handler script, login.php, needs to check the submitted username and password values against the list of valid users. In most cases, you would check the values against a user database. You will learn about database access in PHP in Lessons 19, "Using a MySQL Database," and 20, "Database Abstraction," and for now you can just use a simple array of users who are permitted to use the site. Listing 15.2 shows how to do this.

LISTING 15.2   A Login Processor Script

```php
<?php

session_start();

$passwords = array("chris"   => "letmein",
                   "damon"   => "thisisme",
                   "shelley" => "mypassword",
                   "vanessa" => "opensesame");

if (!$_POST["username"] or !$_POST["password"]) {
  echo "You must enter your username and password";
  exit;
}

if ($_POST["password"] == $passwords[$_POST["username"]]) {
  echo "Login successful";
  $_SESSION["auth_username"] = $_POST["username"];
}
else {
  echo "Login incorrect";
}
?>
```

First, an associative array of passwords is built, using the usernames as keys. The script first checks that both the username and password have been entered and exits immediately if that information is missing.

Then the submitted password is compared to the array element whose key is the submitted username. If the two passwords match, the user is logged in, and the auth_username session variable is initialized. Otherwise, a message is displayed that the login failed.

After a user's session has been validated, he or she can view a protected page without auth.inc interrupting the script's progress.

Encrypting Passwords

In the previous example, the passwords are stored in plain text. You probably suspected that this is not particularly secure; anyone who can view the source code of this script can see the passwords for every user.

 Prying Eyes   Even if your server security is airtight, can you be sure that nobody is looking over your shoulder? You should always try to prevent unencrypted passwords from being displayed onscreen.

The crypt function in PHP provides a simple but effective one-way encryption algorithm. The same kind of encryption is used by htpasswd and even Unix system passwords. To encrypt a password, you pass the password to crypt, along with $salt—another string around which the encryption is based:

```
$crypt_password = crypt($password, $salt);
```

Although the encrypted string cannot be decoded back to the original password, every time you run crypt on the same password with the same salt, the result is the same. Knowing this, you can store only the encrypted version of the password and compare it to the freshly encrypted user input.

Salts If you do not specify a salt, a random one is chosen so subsequent calls to crypt will product different results. A two-character salt, as used by Unix password files and htpasswd, is sufficient.

How a string encoded using crypt looks may vary between different web servers as a system-level encryption library is used. Encrypted passwords are not guaranteed to be portable between different systems. The revised login.php file is shown in Listing 15.3, but be aware that the encrypted passwords shown may not be valid for your system.

LISTING 15.3 A Login Processor Script with Encrypted Passwords

```php
<?php

session_start();

$passwords = array("chris"   => "ZXsDiRf.VBlWQ",
                   "damon"   => "bQLXBRzdBci7M",
                   "shelley" => "KkTH39mVsoclc",
                   "vanessa" => "69SvRIB9QVukk");

if (!$_POST["username"] or !$_POST["password"]) {
  echo "You must enter your username and password";
  exit;
}

$salt = substr($passwords[$_POST["username"]], 0, 2);
if (crypt($_POST["password"], $salt)
        == $passwords[$_POST["username"]]) {
  echo "Login successful";
  $_SESSION["auth_username"] = $_POST["username"];
}
else {
  echo "Login incorrect";
}

?>
```

The `salt` is always found in the first two characters of the encrypted string, so you assign these two characters to `$salt` to use in the call to `crypt`. Other than this, the process is identical to using plain-text passwords.

Usability Considerations

The mechanism you have implemented so far is fairly crude. Any login error results in a message being displayed and the script ending. Even when a login is successful, the flow ends, and the user needs to revisit a protected page directly.

The ideal login mechanism interrupts a hit to a protected web page and displays its login form. Then, after successfully authenticating, it forwards the user to the page he or she was originally trying to access.

One way to add this enhancement is to check the name of the script that the user attempted to access in `auth.inc`; the script name and the query string, if there was one, can be found in `$_SERVER["REQUEST_URI"]`. The login form would then be displayed by `auth.inc` itself, rather than being a separate page.

If you add the following hidden input to the login form, the login processor itself will know which script the user came from, and then you can send the user back to the page he or she was trying to access.

```
<INPUT TYPE="HIDDEN" NAME="destination"
       VALUE="<?php print $_SERVER["REQUEST_URI"];?>">
```

When authentication is successful, rather than print a message to screen, you can forward the user to his or her destination by using the following statement:

```
header("Location: $_POST["destination"]);
```

Summary

In this lesson you have learned ways to protect web pages by using two different authentication methods, including one that is a feature of HTTP. In the next lesson you will see how other HTTP features can be accessed from PHP.

LESSON 16

Communicating with the Web Server

This lesson looks at ways in which PHP can interact with a web server.

HTTP Headers

Every page downloaded from a web server is a result of an exchange of HTTP dialogue. The web browser sends a set of instructions to indicate which page it wants to view, and the server responds with a response that indicates the success of the request, along with various other information that is not displayed directly on the web page.

The following HTTP headers show some of the information that is sent along with a typical web page from a PHP-enabled web server:

```
HTTP/1.1 200 OK
Date: Tue, 14 Dec 2004 21:17:28 GMT
Server: Apache/1.3.29 (Unix) mod_gzip/1.3.26.1a PHP/4.3.9
        mod ssl/2.8.16 OpenSSL/0.0.7c
X-Powered-By: PHP/4.3.9
Connection: close
Content-Type: text/html; charset=iso-8859-1
```

Sending Custom Headers

The PHP function to send a custom HTTP header is header. Let's start by sending a header that does nothing. Any header that begins with X is considered to be for information only; for example, the X-Powered-By header shows that PHP is enabled. To stamp your name in the HTTP headers in your script, you could use the following:

```
header("X-PHP-Author: Chris Newman <chris@lightwood.net>");
```

Of course, there is no reason you should want to send a header like this, other than extreme vanity. A regular user browsing the website would never even see this header!

You have already seen how cookies are sent to a web browser by using the setcookie function. You have also seen that what happens when this function is called is that a Set-Cookie HTTP header is actually sent. The following two PHP statements are therefore equivalent:

```
setcookie("mycookie", "somevalue");
header("Set-Cookie: mycookie=somevalue");
```

Redirection Headers

The header you will send most often is almost certain to be Location, which instructs the web browser to redirect to another URL. You can use this header to change the flow of a website according to events in script. Causing the user's browser to forward to another page is as simple as this:

```
header("Location: anotherpage.php");
```

You can use either a relative or absolute URL in the Location header, so you could even forward the user to another domain, like so:

```
header("Location: http://www.somedomain.com/newpage.php");
```

When a Location header has been sent, you should halt the script immediately, using exit, to make sure that no further output is sent to the browser.

Checking Whether Headers Have Been Sent

As soon as PHP hits the first piece of non-header output in a script, it makes sure all the necessary headers have been sent to the web browser and begins to work on the page itself. All the HTTP headers must be sent at once and must be sent before any of the web page output.

If the headers have already been sent for a script and you attempt to send another, PHP gives an error like this:

```
Warning: Cannot modify header information - headers already
sent by (output started at /home/chris/ public_html/
header.php:4)in /home/chris/ public_html/header.php on line 5
```

In the case of a Location header, you don't need to display anything on the page because the browser goes straight to the new URL. However, you still need to be careful to avoid any HTML output, and particularly white-space, before the script begins; even a single carriage return before the opening <?php tag will prevent you from being able to send custom HTTP headers.

PHP provides the function headers_sent, which you can use to detect whether the HTTP headers have already been sent in that script. The function returns TRUE if headers have been sent and FALSE if it is not too late to send additional custom headers.

The following condition makes sure the headers have not been sent before attempting to perform a redirection:

```
if (!headers_sent()) {
  header("Location: newpage.php");
}
```

Of course, your script would still need to do something else if this condition failed.

Two optional arguments to headers sent allow you to find out the script name and line number where the headers were sent. This is useful if your script is giving an error but you think that the headers have not been sent at that point.

Listing 16.1 attempts to perform a redirect by using a Location header, but if it fails, it displays the reason and an alternative way to get to the destination page. If you run this on your web server, you should add some whitespace or HTML at the top of the script, outside the <?php tags, to make sure the headers are sent prematurely.

LISTING 16.1 Checking Whether Headers Have Been Sent

```php
<?php
$destination = "http://www.lightwood.net/";
if (!headers_sent($filename, $line)) {
  header("Location: $location");
}
else {
  echo "Headers were sent in line $line of $filename <br>";
  echo "<A HREF=\"$destination\">Click here to continue</A>";
}
?>
```

Displaying HTTP Headers

If you want to see which HTTP headers have been or will be sent, you use the headers_list function, which is available in PHP version 5 and above. This function returns an array that contains one header per element.

You can perform a loop on the array returned to grab each value in turn. However, in many cases, all you want to do is see the headers that are being output to check them over, and in this case, passing the array to print_r does the trick:

```php
print_r(headers_list());
```

You need to make sure to put <PRE> tags around this for readability. The following is typical output:

```
Array
(
    [0] => X-Powered-By: PHP/5.0.2
    [1] => Set-Cookie: mycookie=somevalue
    [2] => Content-type: text/html
)
```

Changing Cache Settings

You can use HTTP headers to change the cache settings for a web page, to determine whether a page is completely refreshed each time it is loaded or whether the user's browser—or his or her ISP—will keep a local copy for a period of time to save downloading it from your website again.

You use the Cache-Control header to specify what caching scheme to use for a page. The primary control values for this header are shown in Table 16.1.

TABLE 16.1 Primary Cache-Control Settings

Value	Description
public	May be stored in any web cache.
private	May be saved to the browser's cache but may not be stored in a shared web cache.
no-cache	May not be stored in any cache between the web server and browser.

Usually the reason for overriding the default cache settings is to make sure that a page is fully refreshed every time it is visited.

In most cases, web caches detect that a PHP-generated page with changing content needs to be refreshed frequently, but to make absolutely sure that all your up-to-the-minute content is being displayed correctly around the world, you might want to give it a helping hand.

To make absolutely sure your page will not be cached, using the following statements, which send a number of headers, is generally considered to be the definitive way to prevent caching of any kind:

```
header("Cache-Control: no-store, no-cache, must-revalidate");
header("Cache-Control: post-check=0, pre-check=0", false);
header("Expires: Mon, 26 Jul 1997 05:00:00 GMT");
header("Last-Modified: ". gmdate("D, d M Y H:i:s") . " GMT");
```

A few different headers are used here. Two Cache-Control headers are sent, including a no-cache instruction. You can find more information on the other, less common, Cache-Control settings at www.w3.org/Protocols/rfc2616/rfc2616-sec14.html#sec14.9.

The Expires header tells the browser when a document goes out of date. If you send a historic date in this header, the document will always be considered to be old and need to be refreshed the next time it is viewed.

The Last-Modified header tells the browser how recently the document was modified. When you use the date function, this header always sends the current date, so the browser always thinks it has only just been modified and requests a new copy of the page in full.

> **Session Cache Control**   When a PHP session is started, no-cache headers are automatically sent, along with the other HTTP headers that establish the session. You can use a different cache setting by using the session_cache_limiter function, with one of the values in Table 16.1 as an argument.

Server Environment Variables

Now let's look at the information that PHP allows you to find out from your web server.

The $_SERVER super-global array contains a number of elements that give information about the web server environment during the current page request. To see the full list within the context of a script, you execute this statement at any time:

```
print_r($_SERVER);
```

The examples in this section are common to most web servers. However, some servers may not support all the values shown or may use different names. You can always refer to the output from the previous statement to check which values are available in your script.

Script Information

The name of the current script can be found in $_SERVER["SCRIPT_NAME"]. Knowing this name can be useful if you want to create a form that submits to itself but whose filename you might want to change in the future. You could use the following tag:

```
<FORM ACTION="<?php print $_SERVER["SCRIPT_NAME"];?>"
    METHOD=POST>
```

Similar to SCRIPT_NAME is the REQUEST_URI element, which contains the full uniform resource identifier of the page request. This consists of the full path to the current script, including the question mark and values in the query string, if there are any. The query string is not included as part of the SCRIPT_NAME element, but you can access it on its own as $_SERVER["QUERY_STRING"].

If you want to find the domain name under which a script is running, you can look at $_SERVER["HTTP_HOST"]. Your web server might be set up with several alias domains, and this provides a way to see which domain name a visitor is viewing your pages on.

User Information

The HTTP_USER_AGENT element contains a string that identifies the user's web browser software and operating system. It might look like one of the following:

```
Mozilla/4.0 (compatible; MSIE 6.0; Windows NT 5.1; SV1)
Mozilla/5.0 (Windows; U; Windows NT 5.1; en-US; rv:1.7.5)
              Gecko/20041107 Firefox/1.0
Lynx/2.8.5dev.7 libwww-FM/2.14 SSL-MM/1.4.1 OpenSSL/0.9.7a
```

These three examples correspond to Internet Explorer, Mozilla Firefox, and Lynx, respectively. Notice that both Internet Explorer and Firefox report themselves as Mozilla browsers, so to find out specifically which program a user has, you have to look further into the string.

The following condition can be used to produce different output for Internet Explorer than for Firefox:

```
if (strstr($_SERVER["HTTP_USER_AGENT"], "MSIE")) {
  echo "You are using Internet Explorer";
}
elseif (strstr($_SERVER["HTTP_USER_AGENT"], "Firefox")) {
  echo "You are using Firefox";
}
else {
  echo "You are using some other web browser";
}
```

You may need to use this occasionally because of differences in the browsers' implementations of DHTML or JavaScript.

The REMOTE_ADDR attribute contains the IP address that the hit to the web server came from. It should either be the IP address of the user's computer or the user's ISP's web cache. You might want to use the remote IP address for logging or security.

If the REMOTE_ADDR value is a web cache, the element HTTP_X_FORWARDED_FOR is also present, and it contains the IP address of the user's computer.

If the user has logged in by using basic HTTP authentication, you can also find out his or her username by looking at the value in $_SESSION["REMOTE_USER"].

Server Information

Other elements in $_SERVER allow you to access various values related to the web server configuration.

For instance, $_SERVER["SERVER_NAME"] corresponds to the ServerName Apache directive. This is the primary name of this web server, but not necessarily the domain name the scripts are being accessed from; it might not be the same as $_SERVER["HTTP_HOST"]. Similarly, $_SESSION["SERVER_ADMIN"] holds the webmaster's email address that is set in the ServerAdmin directive.

The SERVER_ADDR and SERVER_PORT elements contain the IP address and port number of the machine the web server is running on. Checking $_SERVER["REQUEST_METHOD"] reveals whether a GET or POST method was used to pass values to the script.

Finally, if you are working on a shared web host or someone else's web server and want to see what web server software version that person is running, you can check $_SERVER["SERVER_SOFTWARE"]. This value is the same as the one transmitted in the Server header at the beginning of this lesson, and it is similar to the following:

```
Apache/1.3.29 (Unix) mod_gzip/1.3.26.1a PHP/4.3.9
mod_ssl/2.8.16 OpenSSL/0.9.7c
```

Summary

In this lesson you have learned how to communicate with a web server. In the next lesson you will learn about filesystem access using PHP.

Lesson 17
Filesystem Access

In this lesson you will learn how to access a web server's filesystem by using PHP and how to read and write files from within a script.

Managing Files

Let's examine how PHP allows you to work with files stored on a web server's hard disk.

File Permissions

Before you can perform any filesystem access from PHP, you have to consider the permission settings for the files you want to work with. This section deals primarily with the file permissions system on Unix/Linux systems, but the same considerations apply to all platforms.

Usually your web server will be running under either the apache or nobody username, yet your web documents and PHP scripts will be owned by your actual system user. Unless the web server user has permissions to access your files, any access attempts will fail.

To grant to all users read-only access to a file, you use the chmod command, which sets the read flag (r) on the file for all users other than the current one (o):

```
$ chmod o+r filename
```

You can also set global read/write permissions on a file by using chmod as follows:

```
$ chmod o+rw filename
```

Refer to man chmod for full details and more examples.

If a file has global permissions, the web server will be able to access it. However, any other user on your system will also have full access to these files. In some situations you might prefer to change the ownership on a file to the apache user rather than grant global write access. The superuser does this by using the chown command:

```
# chown apache filename
```

The PHP function chmod can also be used to alter file permissions. It takes two arguments: a filename and a mode. The mode argument can be either the string type, such as o+rw, or the numeric type, such as 0644, as long as the number is prefixed with a zero.

Using chmod If you are familiar with the system command chmod, you may be used to giving a three-digit number as the mode argument. When run from the shell, chmod assumes that an octal value is given, whether or not it is prefixed with a zero; for example, chmod 644 is the same as chmod 0644. In PHP, however, the leading zero is always required in the argument to chmod.

Getting Information About a File

PHP provides a wide range of functions for getting information about a file on your system. The simplest, and one you may use often, is file_exists, which simply tells you whether there is a file with the given name argument. The file_exists function returns true if any item on the filesystem has the given name, even if it is a directory or a special file type. The argument may contain a path, as shown here:

```
if (file_exists("/home/chris/myfile")) {
  echo "The file exists";
}
else {
  echo "The file does not exist";
}
```

A number of other functions allow you to test certain attributes of a file. These are shown in Table 17.1.

TABLE 17.1   Functions for Testing Attributes of a File

Function	Description
is_executable	Checks whether the file has the executable attribute.
is_readable	Checks whether the file is readable.
is_writeable	Checks whether the file is writeable.
is_link	Checks for a symbolic link.
is_file	Checks for a real file, not a link.

Yet other functions return information about the file itself. These are shown in Table 17.2.

TABLE 17.2   Functions That Find Information About a File

Function	Description
fileatime	Checks the time of the last file access, as a Unix timestamp.
filectime	Checks the time of file inode creation.
filemtime	Checks the time of the last modification to the file.
fileowner	Checks the user ID of the file owner.
filegroup	Checks the group ID of the file.
fileinode	Checks the inode number of the file.
fileperms	Checks the file's permission settings as an octal value (for example, 0644).
filesize	Checks the size of the file in bytes.
filetype	Checks the type of the file (fifo, char, dir, block, link, or file).

Moving and Copying Files

Assuming that you have permission to do so, you can perform a file copy, move, or delete operation from PHP. The functions for these actions are copy, rename, and unlink, respectively.

The copy and rename functions take two arguments—the source and destination filenames—whereas unlink takes a single filename.

 File Paths   You should be particularly careful when performing file operations from PHP, particularly when deleting. You need to always make sure you know what the current working directory is, or give a full path to the target file.

Working with Filenames

The functions basename and dirname provide an easy way to dissect a string into a filename and path, respectively. You might use these functions to find out the base filename when a full path is given or to find the pathname if you want a file created with other files in the same place as a known filename.

The basename function returns everything from the last slash character in the string to the end, whereas dirname returns the portion of the string before this slash.

The realpath function takes a pathname argument and returns its absolute pathname. Any symbolic links in the path are resolved to their actual location on disk, and any references to the current or parent directory using . or .. are removed.

If you want to write to a temporary file, you can use the tempnam function to generate a unique temporary filename. It takes two arguments—a directory name and a filename prefix. The prefix argument is required but can be an empty string. The following statement generates a temporary filename in /tmp with no prefix:

```
$filename = tempnam("/tmp", "");
```

Reading and Writing Files

Now let's see how to read and write files from PHP.

Simple Methods for Reading and Writing Files

PHP provides some simple, high-level functions that can open a file and grab its contents or write data to a file in a single operation.

To read the contents of a file into a string variable, you use `file_get_contents`. The argument is a filename, which can contain a relative or absolute path. The following statement reads a file called `file.txt` into the variable `$data`:

```
$data = file_get_contents("file.txt");
```

An optional second Boolean argument can be set to `true` to search the include path for the given filename. You will see how to configure the include path in Lesson 23, "PHP Configuration."

The function `file_put_contents` simply dumps the contents of a variable to a local file. Its arguments are the filename to write to and the data to write. The following statement writes the value of `$data` to `file.txt`:

```
file_put_contents("file.txt", $data);
```

Lower-Level File Access

The functions `file_get_contents` and `file_put_contents` are high-level functions that perform a number of steps that can be done individually with lower-level PHP functions. Although in many cases reading the entire contents of a file or writing data to a file is the task you will want to perform, PHP provides a flexible way to interface with the filesystem.

All file access begins with a file handler, which is established with the `fopen` function. The arguments to `fopen` are a filename and the mode in which to open the file. The available modes are shown in Table 17.3.

TABLE 17.3 File Mode Arguments to fopen

Mode	Description
r	Opens for reading only from the beginning of the file.
r+	Opens for reading and writing from the beginning of the file.
w	Opens for writing only; overwrites the old file if one already exists.
w+	Opens for writing and reading; overwrites the old file if one already exists.
a	Opens for writing only and appends new data to the end of the file.
a+	Opens for reading and writing at the end of the file.

Each file handler points to a position in the file. You can see from Table 17.3 that when a file is opened by using fopen, the handler always points to either the beginning or the end of the file. As you read or write using that handler, its pointer location moves, and subsequent actions take place from that point in the file.

Let's look at an example where you read the contents of a file a few bytes at a time. By calling fopen with the r mode argument, you create a read-only file handler that initially points to the start of that file.

The fread function reads a fixed number of bytes from a file handler. Its arguments are the file handler and the number of bytes to read. By performing this action in a loop, you can eventually read the entire contents of a file:

```
$fp = fopen("file.txt", "r");
while ($chunk = fread($fp, 100)) {
  echo $chunk;
}
```

This is a very compact statement that checks that fread has succeeded on each pass of the loop. When there is no more data to read, fread returns

FALSE. In fact, by using this loop to output the file to screen, you cannot tell from the result that it was actually done in smaller chunks.

An alternative to fread is fgets, which reads a line of the file at a time. The size argument to fgets has been optional since PHP 4.3 but is shown in these examples for completeness. No more data is read after a carriage return is reached in the file or the specified number of bytes has been read, whichever is sooner.

The following example uses fgets in a loop, assuming that no line in the file is more than 100 characters wide:

```php
$fp = fopen("file.txt", "r");
while ($line = fgets($fp, 100)) {
  echo $line;
}
```

Chopping Strings   Each line read by fgets ends with a newline character. If you want to exclude the newline, you can use the rtrim function on the string to remove it along with any trailing whitespace characters.

When you are finished with a file pointer, you should free up its resources by calling the fclose function:

```php
fclose($fp);
```

Random Access to Files

The file pointer does not have to be moved sequentially through a file; it can be reassigned to any position while the file handle is still open.

To find the current location of the file pointer, you use ftell. An integer is returned—the number of bytes from the start of the file:

```php
$filepos = ftell($fp);
```

To send the file pointer to a specific location, you use the `fseek` function. The following statement places the file pointer 100 bytes from the start, using the file handler `$fp`:

```
fseek($fp, 100);
```

Most often you just want to return the file pointer to the beginning of the file. You could set `fseek` to position zero, or you could just use the built-in function `rewind`:

```
rewind($fp);
```

Writing to a File Pointer

The complementary functions to `fgets` and `fread` to perform write operations on a file pointer are `fputs` and `fwrite`. These functions are actually identical to one another, with the newline character treated just like any other character as they are written to the file.

The following example opens a file and writes to it the current time:

```
$fp = fopen("time.txt", "w");
fwrite($fp, "Data written at ".date("H:i:s"));
fclose($fp);
```

Remember that the `apache` user needs to have write permissions on the directory in order to create a new file.

If you examine the new `time.txt` file, you will see that it does indeed contain the current time.

Working with Data Files

One of the reasons you might need to access the filesystem from PHP is to load data from a structured file format into your script. One of the easiest file formats to use is comma-separated values (CSV).

Although it would appear to be fairly easy to read a line of the file at a time and call `explode` to break up the line where each comma appears, this would not work where data elements in the CSV file contain commas. If you export data from a spreadsheet, columns containing commas are usually enclosed in quotes, so you need quite a complex rule to manipulate the data successfully.

Fortunately, PHP includes the function fgetcsv. It works in a similar way to fgets, except that an array is returned, containing one element for each comma-separated value in the list. The size argument to fgetcsv is optional as of PHP 5.

Often the first line of a CSV file contains the column headings. If you know that this is the case, you should discard the file line before processing the data file. The following example reads a comma-separated data file and dumps each record to screen by using print_r:

```php
$fp = fopen("data.csv", "r");
while ($record = fgetcsv($fp, 1000)) {
  echo $chunk;
}
```

Reading CSV Files   The fgetcsv function requires a line length argument, just like fgets. In the previous example, this has an arbitrary value of 1000, but you should ensure that whatever value you use is larger than the longest line in your data file.

You can also write data to a CSV file without having to manually encode the format. The fputcsv function takes a file handle and an array argument and writes a comma-separated list of the elements in the array.

The optional third and fourth arguments to fputcsv allow you to specify an alternate delimiter and enclosure characters, respectively; the defaults are the comma and double quote characters.

Working with URLs

A powerful feature of PHP is its ability to deal with remote documents in the same way it deals with local files. It is possible to open a file handle or use the high-level filesystem access functions with a URL argument to read a web page from a PHP script.

The following statements are both valid:

```
$page = file_get_contents("http://www.samspublishing.com/");
$fp = fopen("http://www.samspublishing.com/", "r");
```

You cannot write to an HTTP URL by using `file_put_contents` or `fputs`, however.

Working with Directories

Similarly to the way that `fopen` generates a file handle for accessing the contents of a file, you can create a directory handle to view the contents of a directory by using the `opendir` function.

There are just three calls that can be performed on a directory handle—`readdir`, `rewinddir`, and `closedir`—each of which takes a single resource argument.

Each call to `readdir` returns the next file from the directory. The order in which files are returned is the order in which they are stored by the filesystem and cannot be changed. The special items . and .. (the current working directory and its parent) are always returned.

You use `rewinddir` to reset the directory handle to the beginning of the file list at any time, and you close the handle with `closedir` when you are finished with it.

To find the name of the current working directory, you use `getcwd`. No arguments are required, and the full path to the current directory is returned. To change directory, you use `chdir` with a relative or absolute path.

Summary

In this lesson you have learned ways to read and write files on a web server's hard disk. In the next lesson you will learn how to execute local host commands from PHP.

LESSON 18

Host Program Execution

In this lesson you will see how PHP allows you to execute programs on a host system and handle any output that is produced.

Executing Host Programs

PHP can call an external program that resides on a web server in a number of different ways. Let's look at them in the following sections.

The `passthru` Function

The simplest way to run a host command and display the output to screen is by using the `passthru` function. The command passed in as an argument is executed on the web server, and any resulting output is sent to the browser.

The following is a simple example that works on both Unix/Linux and Windows systems:

```
passthru("hostname");
```

The command `hostname` is executed on the host system, and its output is displayed. The `hostname` command finds the system's hostname and displays it.

An optional second argument to `passthru` allows you to find the command's exit code. This is often useful if you want to find out whether a command succeeded—all programs should return an exit code of `zero` on successful completion—or to perform a test on a command that could have several return values.

The most common nonzero return values are 1 for a nonspecific error and 127, which means that the command you attempted to run could not be found. Other error codes specific to a particular program are usually documented.

The following example makes a system call to the hostname command and takes an action, depending on its return code:

```
passthru("hostname", $return);
switch ($return) {
   case 0:    echo "Command completed successfully";
              break;
   case 127:  echo "Command could not be found";
              break;
   default:   echo "Command failed with code $return";
}
```

Using Backticks

The backtick (') character is a handy shortcut that can be used to indicate a system command for execution on the web server itself. A string contained between two backticks is executed, and the response produced by the host system is returned.

The following is equivalent to the passthru example, but it uses the backtick syntax:

```
echo `hostname`;
```

With backticks you are able to assign the result of a host command to a variable, as shown in the following statement:

```
$hostname = `hostname`;
```

In fact, the backtick characters can be used anywhere in a PHP script. They immediately interrupt program execution to call the host command, with the resulting values replaced into the script. The following example shows that the result of a host command can even be used within a condition:

```
if (chop(`hostname`) == "hal9000") {
  echo "Good evening, Dave";
}
```

Because the result from hostname ends with a carriage return—so that the output when run in a command shell looks tidy—the previous example uses chop to make sure that only non-whitespace characters are compared.

> **Exit Codes**   There is no way to obtain an exit code when using backticks. Instead, you should use the exec function, which works just like passthru but returns the command output as a string. The optional second argument can be used to grab the exit code.

Building Command Strings

Commands are passed as arguments to passthru or exec or are simply strings contained in backticks. Therefore, you can build up a command string by using variables or in stages if you want.

Variable substitution takes place within a double-quoted command string, but if the string is enclosed in single quotes, any identifier prefixed with a dollar sign is treated as a shell variable.

Perhaps the strangest looking statement in PHP is one where you execute a command stored in a string by using backticks. This looks as follows:

```
`$cmd`;
```

The variable $cmd could contain any system command and, if you really don't care what the output from the command is, this is valid.

Note, however, that the terminating semicolon is required. A closing backtick closes the host command but does not terminate a PHP statement.

The Host Environment

Now let's look at how PHP interacts with the web server's host environment.

Detecting the Host Platform

Because different types of systems have different sets of host commands available, if you are writing a script that could potentially be executed on different platforms, it's useful to detect what kind of web server is being used.

The constant PHP_OS contains a string that represents the operating system. The most common reason for checking this is to find out whether a script is running on a Windows platform—after all, most Unix-like systems, and even Mac OS, behave in a very similar way.

The value of PHP_OS on a Windows web server could be Windows, WINNT, or WIN32, and in the future, other values may come into existence. Therefore, to test for a Windows platform, you should perform a non-case-sensitive comparison on the first three characters of the string. The following condition shows just one of the ways you can do this:

```
if (strtoupper(substr(PHP_OS, 0, 3)) == "WIN") { ... }
```

 Darwin   Be cautious to check only that the value of PHP_OS *begins* with WIN, as modern versions of Mac OS report themselves as Darwin.

Environment Variables

The $_ENV super-global contains an element for each environment variable present. *Environment variables* are values from the underlying operating system, and those available to PHP are from the environment in which PHP and your web server is running.

The PATH environment variable provides your system with a list of locations to search for an executable program. Each location is checked in turn until the program is found or there are no more locations left to try, when an error occurs.

Finding the current value of the path is as simple as using the following statement:

```
echo $_ENV["PATH"];
```

On a Unix/Linux system it may look like the following:

```
/bin:/usr/bin:/usr/X11R6/bin:/home/chris/bin
```

On a Windows system, however, it may look like this:

```
C:\WINDOWS\system32;C:\WINDOWS
```

Notice that the format is considerably different for the different operating systems. The Unix/Linux version uses colons to separate the locations and forward slashes in pathnames, and the Windows version uses semicolons and backslashes. For this reason, PHP provides the host-specific constants DIRECTORY_SEPARATOR and PATH_SEPARATOR, which enable you to find the appropriate symbols to use for each of these.

In many cases, resetting the PATH value is specific to the underlying platform; for instance, even if you use the correct PATH_SEPARATOR constant, C:/WINDOWS will not exist on a Linux server. However, this allows you to add the current working directory, or one relative to it, to the path fairly easily.

The following example adds the directory bin, relative to the current location, to the start of the system path:

```
$newpath = getcwd() . DIRECTORY_SEPARATOR . "bin" .
           PATH_SEPARATOR . $_ENV["PATH"];
putenv("PATH=$newpath");
```

The putenv function takes a single argument in which an environment variable is assigned its new value. This change is not permanent, and the new value is remembered only until the script ends.

Time Zones

The TZ environment variable contains the server's time zone setting. By overriding this value, you can display the time in another part of the world without needing to know the correct offset or perform any date arithmetic.

Most major cities or regions of the world have a value for TZ that is easy to remember or work out (for instance, Europe/London, US/Pacific). It can also be a value relative to Greenwich Mean Time or some other common time zone, such as GMT-8 or EST. On most systems, you can find the available time zones by looking at the items in /usr/share/zoneinfo.

The script in Listing 18.1 displays the current time in several locations around the globe.

LISTING 18.1 Using the TZ Environment Variable to Change Time Zone

```php
<?php
$now = time();
$original_tz = $_ENV["TZ"];

echo "The time now is " . date("H:i:s", $now) . "<br>";

putenv("TZ=US/Pacific");
echo "The time on the US West Coast is " .
        date("H:i:s", $now) . "<br>";

putenv("TZ=Europe/Paris");
echo "The time in France is " . date("H:i:s", $now) , "<hr>"j

putenv("TZ=Australia/Sydney");
echo "The time in Sydney is " . date("H:i:s", $now) . "<br>";

putenv("TZ=Asia/Tokyo");
echo "The time in Tokyo is " . date("H:i:s", $now) . "<br>";

putenv("TZ=$original_tz");
?>
```

Note that Listing 18.1 begins by storing the current time zone value so that it can be restored after you are done changing the value.

> **Storing the Time**   The timestamp is saved to $now at the start of Listing 18.1 so that the same value can be passed to each date function. Although the second argument to date can be omitted, if it is omitted, it is possible that the script execution could take place as a second ticks over, which would produce confusing output.

Security Considerations

Hopefully you have realized that having on your web server a script that is able to execute host program commands is not always a good idea. In fact, in Lesson 24, "PHP Security," you will learn how you can use PHP's Safe Mode to place restrictions on host program execution.

To end this lesson, you will learn how to make sure that host program execution is always done safely.

Escaping Shell Commands

Consider the script in Listing 18.2, which creates a web form interface to the finger command.

LISTING 18.2   Calling the finger Command from a Web Form

```
<FORM ACTION="finger.php" METHOD="POST">
<INPUT NAME="username" SIZE=10>
<INPUT TYPE="SUBMIT" VALUE="Finger username">
</FORM>
<?php
if ($_POST["username"]) {
  $cmd = "finger {$_POST['username']}";
  echo "<PRE>" . `$cmd` . "</PRE>";
}
?>
```

If you run this script in your browser and enter a username, the `finger`
information will be displayed.

However, if you instead enter a semicolon followed by another command—for instance, `;ls`—the `finger` command is run without an argument and then the second command you entered is executed. Similar
trickery can be produced using other symbols, depending on your web
server platform.

This is clearly not a good thing. You might think that only limited damage
could be done through running processes as the same user as the web
server; however, many serious exploits can take advantage of this behavior. A malicious user could issue a command such as `wget` or `lynx` to
install a hostile program on your server's hard disk and then run it. This
could be a `rootkit` to attempt to take advantage of other server vulnera-
bilities, or it could be a script to launch a denial-of-service attack by eat-
ing up all your system resources. However you look at it, giving
anonymous users this kind of access to your web server is bad news.

To protect yourself against this kind of attack, you should use the
`escapeshellcmd` function. Any characters that may be used to fool the
shell into executing a command other than the one intended are prefixed
with a backslash. This way, undesirable characters actually become arguments to the command.

To make Listing 18.2 safe, the statement that builds `$cmd` should be
changed to the following:

```
$cmd = escapeshellcmd("finger {$_POST['username']}");
```

Now, entering `;ls` into the form will result in the command executed
being `finger \; ls`—actually attempting to find users called `;` or `ls` on
your system.

Summary

In this lesson you have learned how to safely run host commands on your
web server from PHP and deal with the output they produce. In the next
lesson you will learn about database access in PHP using MySQL.

LESSON 19

Using a MySQL Database

In this lesson you will learn how to access a MySQL database from PHP. The pairing of PHP and MySQL is so popular and powerful that it is quite rare to find PHP being used without MySQL—or at least some other database back end.

Using MySQL

This lesson assumes that you already have MySQL installed on your web server and that PHP has the MySQL module loaded. For information on installing MySQL, see http://dev.mysql.com/doc/mysql/en/Installing.html, and to learn how to activate MySQL support in PHP, refer to Lesson 23, "PHP Configuration."

> **Further Reading**   To learn about the MySQL database, read *Sams Teach Yourself MySQL in 24 Hours* by Julie Meloni. Or for a quick SQL language guide, refer to *Sams Teach Yourself SQL in 10 Minutes* by Ben Forta.

PHP 5 introduced the `mysqli` extension, which can take advantage of new functionality in MySQL version 4.1 and higher and can also be used in an object-oriented manner. This book concentrates on the classic `mysql` extension, because it is still the version offered by many web hosting providers and remains available in PHP 5.

Generally speaking, if you want to use `mysqli` instead of the classic `mysql` extension described in this lesson, most function names are prefixed `mysqli` rather than `mysql`, but they behave in a similar way. Refer to the online documentation at www.php.net/mysqli for more information.

Connecting to a MySQL Database

You can connect to a MySQL database by using the `mysql_connect` function. Three arguments define your connection parameters—the hostname, username, and password. In many cases, the MySQL server will be running on the same machine as PHP, so this value is simply `localhost`. A typical `mysql_connect` statement may look like the following:

```
$db = mysql_connect("localhost", "chris", "mypassword");
```

> **Database Hostnames** Because MySQL uses host-based authentication, you must provide the correct hostname—one that allows a connection to be made. For instance, your MySQL server may be running on www.yourdomain.com but it might only be configured to accept connections to `localhost`.
>
> Unless you are sure that the MySQL server is running somewhere else, the hostname to use is almost always `localhost`.

The `mysql_connect` function returns a database link identifier, which was assigned to `$db` in the previous example. This resource is used as an argument to the other MySQL functions.

Notice that the connection parameters given to `mysql_connect` do not include a database name. In fact, selecting the database is a separate step after you are connected to a MySQL server; to do it, you use the `mysql_select_db` function. For example, the following statement selects `mydb` as the current database:

```
mysql_select_db("mydb", $db);
```

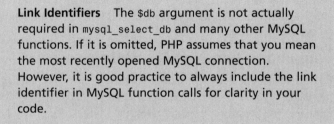

Link Identifiers   The `$db` argument is not actually required in `mysql_select_db` and many other MySQL functions. If it is omitted, PHP assumes that you mean the most recently opened MySQL connection. However, it is good practice to always include the link identifier in MySQL function calls for clarity in your code.

After `mysql_select_db` has been called, every subsequent SQL statement passed to MySQL will be performed on the selected database.

When you are finished using MySQL in a script, you close the connection and free up its resources by using `mysql_close`, like this:

```
mysql_close($db);
```

Executing SQL Statements

The function to pass a SQL statement to MySQL is `mysql_query`. It takes two arguments—the query itself and an optional link identifier.

The following code executes a CREATE TABLE SQL statement on the MySQL database for `$db`:

```
$sql = "CREATE TABLE mytable (col1 INT, col2 VARCHAR(10))";
mysql_query($sql, $conn);
```

If you run a script that contains these statements in your web browser and check your MySQL database, you will find that a new table called `mytable` has been created.

All types of SQL statement can be executed through `mysql_query`, whether they alter the data in some way or fetch a number of rows.

Commands That Change a Database

Earlier in this lesson you saw an example of a CREATE TABLE statement. Other Data Definition Language (DDL) statements can be executed in a similar fashion, and, provided that no errors are encountered, they perform silently. You will learn about error handling later in this lesson.

When executing a DELETE, INSERT, or UPDATE statement—a subset of SQL known as the Database Manipulation Language (DML)—a number of rows in the table may be affected by the query. To find out how many rows are actually affected, you can use the mysql_affected_rows function. The following example shows how to do this with a simple UPDATE statement:

```
$sql = "UPDATE mytable SET col2 = 'newvalue' WHERE col1 > 5";
mysql_query($sql, $conn);
echo mysql_affected_rows($conn) . " row(s) were updated";
```

The argument to mysql_affected_rows is the database link identifier, and a call to this function returns the number of rows affected by the most recent query. The number of rows affected by this UPDATE statement is not necessarily the number of rows matching the WHERE clause. MySQL does not update a row if the new value is the same as the one already stored.

> **Deleting All Rows**   If you execute a DELETE statement with no WHERE clause, the number returned by mysql_affected_rows is zero, regardless of the number of rows actually deleted. MySQL simply empties the table rather than delete each row in turn, so no count is available.

Fetching Queried Data

The SELECT statement should return one or more rows from the database, so PHP provides a set of functions to make this data available within a script. In order to work with selected data, you must assign the result from mysql_query to a result resource identifier, as follows:

```
$res = mysql_query($sql, $db);
```

You cannot examine the value of $res directly. Instead, you pass this value to other functions to retrieve the database records.

You can use the function mysql_result to reference a data item from a specific row and column number in the query result. This is most useful when your query will definitely only return a single value—for instance, the result of an aggregate function.

The following example performs a SUM operation on the elements in a table column and displays the resulting value onscreen:

```
$sql = "SELECT SUM(col1) FROM mytable";
$res = mysql_query($sql, $conn);
echo mysql_result($res, 0, 0);
```

The three arguments to mysql_result are the result resource identifier, a row number, and a column number. Numbering for both rows and columns begins at zero, so this example finds the first row in the first column in the result set. In fact, because of the nature of aggregate functions, you can be sure that there will always be only a single row and column in the result of this query, even if there are no records in the table. An attempt to access a row or column number that does not exist will result in an error.

The function mysql_num_rows returns the number of rows found by the query, and you can use this value to create a loop with mysql_result to examine every row in the result. The following code shows an example of this:

```
$sql = "SELECT col1, col2 FROM mytable";
$res = mysql_query($sql, $db);
for ($i=0; $i < mysql_num_rows($res); $i++) {
  echo "col1 = " . mysql_result($res, $i, 0);
  echo ", col2 = " . mysql_result($res, $i, 1) . "<br>";
}
```

With the query used in this example, because the column positions of col1 and col2 are known, you can use mysql_result with a numeric argument to specify each one in turn.

> **Field Names**   You can use a string for the column
> argument to `mysql_result`; in this case, you need to
> give the column's name. This behavior is particularly
> useful in SELECT * queries, where the order of
> columns returned may not be known, and in queries
> where the number of columns returned is not easily
> manageable.

Fetching Full Rows of Data

PHP provides a convenient way to work with more than one item from a
selected row of data at a time. By using `mysql_fetch_array`, you can create an array from the query result that contains one element for each column in the query.

When you call `mysql_fetch_array` on a result resource handle for the
first time, an array is returned that contains one element for each column
in the first row of the data set. Subsequent calls to `mysql_fetch_array`
cause an array to be returned for each data row in turn. When there is no
more data left to be fetched, the function returns FALSE.

You can build a very powerful loop structure by using `mysql_fetch_`
`array`, as shown in the following example:

```
$sql = "SELECT col1, col2 FROM mytable";
$res = mysql_query($sql, $conn);
while ($row = mysql_fetch_array($res)) {
   echo "col1 = " . $row["col1"];
   echo ", col2 = " . $row["col2"] . "<br>";
}
```

Each row of data is fetched in turn, and in each pass of the loop, the entire
row of data is available in the array structure, without any further function
calls being necessary.

The array contains the row's data, using elements with both numeric and
associative indexes. In the previous example, because you know that col1
is the first column selected, $row["col1"] and $row[0] contain the same
value.

This mechanism provides a method of sequential access to every row returned by a query. Random access is also available, and by using the function `mysql_data_seek`, you can specify a row number to jump to before the next `mysql_fetch_array` is performed.

To jump to the tenth row, you would use the following (remember that the numbering begins at zero, not one):

```
mysql_data_seek($res, 9);
```

It therefore follows that to reset the row position to the start of the data set, you should seek row zero:

```
mysql_data_seek($res, 0);
```

If you attempt to call `mysql_data_seek` with a row number that is higher than the total number of rows available, an error occurs. You should check the row number against the value of `mysql_num_rows` to ensure that it is valid.

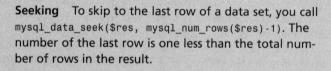

Seeking   To skip to the last row of a data set, you call `mysql_data_seek($res, mysql_num_rows($res)-1)`. The number of the last row is one less than the total number of rows in the result.

However, the result can usually be achieved more easily by specifying reverse sorting in an ORDER BY clause in your SQL and selecting the first row instead.

Debugging SQL

When a PHP call to the MySQL interface encounters a database error, the warnings displayed are not always as helpful as you might hope. In the following sections you will find out how to make the most of MySQL's error reporting to debug errors at the database level.

SQL Errors

When there is an error in a SQL statement, it is not reported right away. You should check the return value from `mysql_query` to determine whether there was a problem—it is NULL if the query has failed for any reason. This applies to DDL and DML statements as well as to SELECT queries.

The following example tries to perform an invalid SQL statement (the table name is missing from the DELETE command):

```
$sql = "DELETE FROM";
$res = mysql_query($sql, $db);
if (!$res) {
  echo "There was an SQL error";
  exit;
}
```

If you want to find out why a call to `mysql_query` failed, you must use the `mysql_error` and `mysql_errno` functions to retrieve the underlying MySQL warning text and error code number. A link resource argument can be provided but is required only if you have two or more open MySQL connections in the script:

```
if (!$res) {
  echo "Error " . mysql_errno() . " in SQL ";
  echo "<PRE>$sql</PRE>";
  echo mysql_error();
  exit;
}
```

> **Debugging SQL**   When you're debugging SQL, it is useful to see the query that was attempted alongside the error message, particularly if your query uses variable substitutions. This is easy to do if the query is stored in a variable—such as `$sql` used throughout this lesson—rather than given directly as an argument to `mysql_query`.

If you do not trap SQL errors in script, PHP will continue to execute until an attempt is made to use the failed result resource. You will see an error message similar to the following if, for instance, `mysql_result` is called with an invalid `$res` value:

```
Warning: mysql_result(): supplied argument is not a valid
MySQL result resource in /home/chris/mysql.php on line 8
```

This error does not give any indication of what the problem was, or even when in the script it occurred. The line number given is the line of the `mysql_result` call, not `mysql_query`, so you have to search upward in the script to find the root of the problem.

Connection Errors

If an error occurs during connection to a MySQL database, a PHP error is displayed onscreen, similar to the following, which were caused by an invalid password and a mistyped hostname, respectively:

```
Warning: mysql_connect(): Access denied for user
'root'@'localhost'
  (using password: YES) in /home/chris/connect.php on line 3

Warning: mysql_connect(): Unknown MySQL server host
'local-host'
  (1) in /home/chris/connect.php on line 3
```

These warnings are generated by PHP and are adequately descriptive. If you want, you can view the actual MySQL error message and error code by using `mysql_error` and `mysql_errno`.

For instance, if you have stopped PHP warnings from being displayed onscreen—you will learn how to do this in Lesson 23—it might be useful to output this information or write it to a log file. You can detect that the connection attempt failed because the link resource is NULL.

The following code checks that a connection has been successful before continuing, and it displays the reason for failure, if appropriate:

```
$db = mysql_connect("localhost", "chris", "mypassword");
if (!$db) {
  echo "Connection failed with error " .
              mysql_errno() . "<br>";
  echo "Warning: " . mysql_error();
  exit;
}
```

> **Passwords** Neither the PHP warning nor the message from mysql_error contains the password used when the reason for failure is an invalid logon attempt.

Summary

In this lesson you have learned how to use PHP's interface to the MySQL database system. In the next lesson you will learn how PHP can communicate with different database back ends by using a database abstraction layer.

LESSON 20
Database Abstraction

In this lesson you will learn how to access different databases from PHP, using a single interface. Database abstraction is a very powerful technique; it allows you to write scripts for a nonspecific database back end, which you can then easily port simply by changing the connection parameters.

The PEAR DB Class

Many different database abstraction layers are available for PHP, but the one you will learn how to use in this lesson is the PEAR DB class. In Lesson 25, "Using PEAR," you will find out more about PEAR—the PHP Extension and Application Repository—and some other useful classes it contains.

The DB class implements database abstraction, using PHP's database extensions, and it currently supports the extensions shown in Table 20.1.

TABLE 20.1 PHP Database Extensions supported by the PEAR DB Class

Extension	Database
dbase	dBase (.dbf)
fbsql	FrontBase
ibase	Firebird/Interbase
ifx	Informix
msql	Mini SQL

Extension	Database
mssql	Microsoft SQL Server
mysql	MySQL
mysqli	MySQL 4.1 and higher
oci8	Oracle versions 7, 8, and 9
odbc	ODBC
pgsql	PostgreSQL
sqlite	SQLite
Sybase	Sybase

> **DB Class Documentation** The online documentation for the PEAR DB class can be found at http://pear. php.net/package/DB.

Installing the DB Class

To check whether the DB class is installed on your web server, you can run the following command to display a list of installed packages:

```
$ pear list
```

If you need to install the DB class, you run the following command:

```
$ pear install DB
```

Note that you need to be an admin to install a PEAR class, so if you are using a shared web hosting service, you might need to contact your system administrator.

Because the underlying PHP extensions are used, no additional database drivers are needed to communicate with each type of database from the DB class.

> **Further Reading** To learn about the MySQL database, read *Sams Teach Yourself MySQL in 24 Hours* by Julie Meloni. Or, for a quick SQL language guide, refer to *Sams Teach Yourself SQL in 10 Minutes* by Ben Forta.

Data Source Names

To connect to a database through the DB class, you need to construct a valid data source name (DSN), which is a single string that contains all the parameters required to connect and is formed in a similar manner to a URL that you might use to access a protected web page or FTP server.

The following DSN can be used to connect to a MySQL database running on localhost:

```
mysql://chris:mypassword@localhost/mydb
```

The components of this DSN are the database back-end type (mysql), username (chris), password (mypassword), host (localhost), and database name (mydb).

The full syntax definition for a DSN is as follows, and the components that it can be constructed from are given in Table 20.2.

```
phptype(dbsyntax)://username:password@protocol+hostspec/
database?option=value
```

TABLE 20.2   Components of a DSN

Component	Description
phptype	Database back-end protocol to use (for example, mysql, oci8)
dbsyntax	Optional parameters related to SQL syntax; for ODBC, should contain the database type (for example, access, mssql)
username	Username for database login

Component	Description
password	Password for database login
protocol	Connection protocol (for example, `tcp`, `unix`)
hostspec	Host specification, either *hostname* or *hostname:port*
database	Database name
option	Additional connection options; multiple options are separated by &

As shown in the first example of connecting to MySQL, not every component of the DSN is required. The exact syntax depends on what information your database back end needs.

For instance, a connection to SQLite—which requires no `username`, `password`, or `hostspec`—would look like the following:

```
sqlite:///path/to/dbfile
```

On the other hand, a connection to a PostgreSQL server that is not running on a standard port number would require something more complex like this:

```
pgsql://username:password@tcp(hostname:port)/dbname
```

 Database Types The database type values for the `phptype` argument are the values shown in the first column of Table 20.1.

Using the DB Class

To begin using the DB class in scripts, you simply include it by using the following statement:

```
include "DB.php";
```

To make a connection to a database, you call the connect method on the
DB class, giving your DSN as the argument:

```
$db = DB::connect($dsn);
```

The $db return value is an object on which the DB class methods can be
invoked to perform different types of database operation.

Database Objects   Note that you cannot create a
new instance of a DB object by using the new keyword.
You must call DB::connect to begin a new database
session.

If the database connection fails, the return value is a DB_Error object,
which you can analyze by using the isError and getMessage methods.
The following code shows a database connection attempt with error
checking:

```
$db = DB::connect($dsn);
if (DB::isError($db)) {
  echo "Connection error: " . $db->getMessage();
  exit;
}
```

The function isError returns true only if the argument passed is a
DB_Error object, which indicates a problem of some kind with the database connection. You can then call the getMessage method on the
DB_Error object to retrieve the actual error message from the database
server.

Connection Errors $db is assigned an object value of
some kind, whether or not the connection is successful. Its value will never be NULL or FALSE.

Performing a Query

To execute a SQL query through the DB class, you use the query method. The return value depends on the type of query being executed, but in the event of any error, a DB_Error object is returned, and the error can be detected and diagnosed in the same way as can connection errors.

The following example executes the query stored in $sql with error checking:

```
$res = $db->query($sql);
if (DB::isError($res)) {
  echo "Query error " . $res->getMessage();
  exit;
}
```

If the query submitted is an INSERT, UPDATE, or DELETE statement, the return value is the constant DB_OK. You can find out the number of rows affected by the statement by calling the affectedRows method on the database object itself, as shown in the following example:

```
$sql = "UPDATE mytable SET col2 = 'newvalue' WHERE col1 > 5";
$res = $db->query($sql);
echo $db->affectedRows(). " row(s) were affected";
```

Retrieving Selected Data

If you issue a SELECT statement, the return value from the query is a DB_Result object, which can then be used to access records from the result data set.

To view the number of rows and columns in the data set, you use the numRows and numCols methods, respectively, as in this example:

```
$sql = "SELECT * FROM mytable";
$res = $db->query($sql);
echo "Query found " . $res->numRows . " row(s) ".
     "and " . $res->numCols . " column(s)";
```

You can use the fetchRow method on a DB_Result object to return a row of data at a time in an array structure. The result pointer is then increased so that each subsequent call to fetchRow returns the next row of data, in order. The following code shows how you can fetch all the rows returned by a query by using fetchRow in a loop:

```
$sql = "SELECT col1, col2 FROM mytable";
$res = $db->query($sql);
while ($row = $res->fetchRow()) {
   echo "col1 = " . $row[0] . ", ";
   echo "col2 = " . $row[1] . "<br>";
}
```

In this example, elements of $row are numerically indexed, beginning at zero. Because the selected columns are specified in the SELECT statement, the order is known and you can be sure that $row[0] contains the value of col1.

You can give an optional argument to fetchRow to change the array indexing. The default, which causes a numerically indexed array to be created, is DB_FETCHMODE_ORDERED. By specifying DB_FETCHMODE_ASSOC, you cause an associative array to be created, using the column names as keys.

You could use the following loop to reproduce the previous example, instead using an associative array of the fetched values:

```
while ($row = $res->fetchRow(DB_FETCHMODE_ASSOC)) {
   echo "col1 = " . $row["col1"] . ", ";
   echo "col2 = " . $row["col2"] . "<br>";
}
```

If you prefer, you can use the fetchRow method to create an object structure rather than an array, by passing the argument DB_FETCHMODE_OBJECT. The following loop is equivalent to the previous two examples, but it uses the object method:

```
while ($row = $res->fetchRow(DB_FETCHMODE_OBJECT)) {
   echo "col1 = " . $row->col1. ", ";
   echo "col2 = " . $row->col2 . "<br>";
}
```

> **Fetch Modes**   Which fetch mode you use usually depends on your preference. The associative array and object structures usually create mode-readable code. However, where optimal performance is essential, you should try to use DB_FETCHMODE_ORDERED.

Query Shortcuts

If a query will return only a single row and column—for instance, the result of a single aggregate function—you can use the getOne method to quickly execute the query and return the result. A string query argument is supplied, and the database result is returned:

```
$sum = $db->getOne("SELECT sum(col1) FROM mytable");
```

Other shortcut methods are available, including getRow, to execute a query and return a whole row, and getAll, to execute a query and return the entire dataset as an array. Refer to the documentation for a full list of functions.

Database Portability Issues

By using database abstraction, you can write database-driven code that should be able to work with a multitude of back ends, simply by changing the DSN used to connect to the database.

However, not all database systems are the same, so you need to consider the design of database tables and SQL statements in order to make sure that your code is as widely supported as possible.

The most important consideration is to make sure that your SQL is written for the lowest common subset of the SQL language available to all the database back ends you want to be compatible with. For example, SQL that contains subqueries will not work with MySQL 4.0 or earlier. Similarly, you should avoid SQL commands that are specific to certain database systems, such as LIMIT or CREATE SEQUENCE.

Portability Modes

The DB class includes some portability mode settings that can ease the transition from one database back end to another. These modes are indicated by a series of constants, shown in Table 20.3, that you can set by using the setOption method with the required options, combined with a logical OR operator. The following statement shows an example:

```
$db->setOption('portability',
    DB_PORTABILITY_ERRORS ¦ DB_PORTABILITY_NUMROWS);
```

TABLE 20.3 Portability Mode Constants

Constant	Mode
DB_PORTABILITY_ALL	Turns on all portability features
DB_PORTABILITY_NONE	Turns off all portability features
DB_PORTABILITY_DELETE_COUNT	Forces a count to take place in a DELETE statement with no WHERE clause, with WHERE 1=1 appended to the statement
DB_PORTABILITY_ERRORS	Increases consistency of error reporting between different database systems
DB_PORTABILITY_LOWERCASE	Forces conversion of names of tables and columns to lowercase
DB_PORTABILITY_NULL_TO_EMPTY	Converts fetched NULL values to empty strings; some databases do not distinguish these
DB_PORTABILITY_NUMROWS	Enables the numRows method to work correctly in Oracle
DB_PORTABILITY_RTRIM	Forces trailing whitespace to be trimmed from fetched data

Working with Quotes

You can use the DB method quoteSmart to enclose a value in quotation marks so that it can be safely inserted into a column. String values are enclosed in quotes, and any characters that need to be delimited are automatically taken care of.

The following example builds a SQL statement by using quoteSmart to ensure that the apostrophe in the string does not interfere:

```
$sql    = "INSERT INTO phrases (phrase) " .
          "VALUES ( " . $db->quoteSmart($text) . " )";
```

The following is the value of $sql when the previous statement is executed, using the MySQL driver:

```
INSERT INTO phrases (phrase)
VALUES ( 'Let\'s get ready to rumble' )
```

The output and the delimiting rules used depend on the database you are connected to.

Sequences

The way sequences are implemented in different database engines varies considerably. In MySQL, for instance, you use the AUTO_INCREMENT attribute on a table column, and in SQL Server it is called an IDENTITY field. In Oracle you use CREATE SEQUENCE to create a database object that tracks the sequence value independently of any table.

The DB class uses its own set of functions to manage sequences so that using any kind of auto-incrementing field does not tie your code to one particular database back end.

> **Sequences** If your back-end database supports
> CREATE SEQUENCE, that functionality will be used.
> Otherwise, the DB class emulates the sequence by
> using a table that holds the sequence value, and it
> performs an increment each time the sequence is
> accessed.

To create a new sequence, you use the `createSequence` method on a database object, with a unique sequence identifier. After the sequence has been created, the `nextId` method can be called with that identifier to return the next sequential value.

The following example creates a sequence called `order_number` and displays the first sequence value:

```
$db->createSequence("order_number");
echo $db->nextId("order_number");
```

Subsequent calls to `nextId` for this sequence return incremental values.

To drop a sequence when you no longer have a use for it, you call the `dropSequence` method.

Query Limits

MySQL implements the `LIMIT` keyword in SQL statements, which you can use to restrict the number of rows returned by a query. This is nonstandard SQL, and other database systems do not include this feature.

The DB class includes the `limitQuery` method, which you can use to emulate the `LIMIT` clause in a SQL statement for maximum compatibility. This method is called in the same way as a query, but it takes two additional arguments: to specify the starting row and number of rows to be returned.

The following example returns five rows from the query's data set, beginning at row 11 (where row numbering begins at zero):

```
$res = $db->limitQuery("SELECT * FROM mytable", 10, 5);
```

Summary

In this lesson you have learned how to write database-driven PHP scripts by using a database abstraction layer. In the next lesson you will learn how to write and run command scripts by using PHP.

LESSON 21

Running PHP on the Command Line

Although PHP was conceived as a tool for creating dynamic web pages, because the PHP language is very powerful, it has also become popular for writing command scripts and even desktop programs.

In this lesson you will learn how to write PHP for use from the command line and create your own command scripts.

The Command-Line Environment

In order to use PHP from the command line, you need to have a PHP executable installed on your system. When running in a web environment, PHP is usually installed as an Apache module, but it is also possible to build a standalone program called php that can be used as a command-line interface (CLI).

Differences Between CLI and CGI Binaries

Beginning in version 4.2, PHP started to differentiate between binary programs intended for CGI and those for CLI use. Both executables provide the same language interpreter, but the CLI version includes the following changes to make it more suitable for command-line use:

- No HTTP headers are written in the output.

- Error messages do not contain HTML formatting.

- The max_execution_time value is set to zero, meaning that the script can run for an unlimited amount of time.

To find out whether a php binary is a CGI or CLI version, you can run it with the -v switch to see its version information. For instance, the following output is from the CLI version PHP 5.0.3:

```
PHP 5.0.3 (cli) (built: Dec 15 2004 08:07:57)
Copyright (c) 1997-2004 The PHP Group
Zend Engine v2.0.3, Copyright (c) 1998-2004 Zend Technologies
```

The value in parentheses after the version number indicates the Server Application Programming Interface (SAPI) that is in use. You can also find this value dynamically in a script by looking at the return value from the function php_sapi_name.

Windows Distributions The Windows distributions of PHP 4.2 included two binaries—the CGI version was called php.exe, and the CLI binary was php-cli.exe. For PHP 4.3, both were called php.exe, but they were found in folders called cli and cgi, respectively.

For PHP 5 and higher, php.exe is the CLI version, and now the CGI binary is named php-cgi.exe. A new php-win.exe CLI binary is also included that runs silently—that is, the user doesn't need to open a command prompt window.

PHP Shell Scripts on Linux/Unix

On a Linux/Unix platform, a *shell script* is simply a text file that contains a series of instructions that are to be processed by a specific language interpreter. The simplest shell interpreter is the Bourne Shell, sh, although these days it has been superseded by the Bourne Again Shell, bash, which is fully compatible with sh but also includes other useful features.

Because the command language available in most command shells is very restrictive and often requires calls to external programs, PHP is not only a more powerful language, suitable for many tasks, but its built-in features also usually give better performance than the standard system tools.

PHP Location   The php executable is usually installed to /usr/local/bin or /usr/bin, depending on whether it was installed from source or a binary package, but your actual location may vary. Try typing which php to find the location if you do not know it.

All shell scripts must begin with the characters #!, followed by the path to the command interpreter that is to be used. For a traditional shell script, this would look like the following:

```
#!/bin/sh
```

However, for a PHP script, the first line would be

```
#!/usr/local/bin/php
```

Hash Bang   The most widely used pronunciation for the character sequence #!, found at the start of a shell script, is "hash bang," although sometimes it is also referred to as "shebang."

The file permissions on a shell script must allow the file to be executed. To set execute permission for the owner of the file, you use the following command:

```
$ chmod u+x myscript.php
```

If your script is to be run by any system user, the command to set global execute permission is as follows:

```
$ chmod a+x myscript.php
```

If the execute bit is not set, you can still run a file that contains a series of PHP commands through the PHP interpreter by invoking php with a filename argument. The following two commands are identical to one another (the -f switch can be used for clarity but is not required):

```
$ php myscript.php
$ php -f myscript.php
```

> **Script Names**   There are no naming requirements for any type of shell script. However, it is useful to retain the .php extension so that the filename indicates a PHP script. Bourne shell scripts sometimes have the file extension .sh but often are command names with no file extension at all.

PHP Command Scripts on Windows

Windows does not allow an alternate command interpreter to be used in a batch script, so to execute a PHP script under Windows, you have to pass a filename argument to php.exe. The -f switch is optional, so the following two commands are identical to one another:

```
> php.exe myscript.php
> php.exe -f myscript.php
```

> **Batch Scripts**   If you want, you can create a simple batch script to invoke php.exe with the correct filename argument so that you can run your script by using a single command.
>
> To do so, you create a file named myscript.bat that contains the command php.exe, followed by your script name. You can then run that script by simply entering myscript at the command prompt.

Embedding PHP Code

Just as when it is used in the web environment, PHP code in a command script needs to be embedded. Any text that does not appear inside <?php tags is sent straight to the output.

Because you usually want to create a script that is entirely made up of PHP code, you must remember to begin every PHP shell script with a

<?php tag. However, the embedded nature of PHP means you could create a PHP script that generates only certain elements within a largely static text file.

Writing Scripts for the Command Line

The PHP language provides certain functionality that is particularly useful for writing command-line scripts. You will rarely, if ever, use these features in the web environment, but they are described in the following sections.

Character Mode Output

When you're producing web output, you use the <br> tag to produce a simple line break in the output. When it is sent to a web page, the newline character, \n, causes a line break in the HTML source, but it is not visible in the rendered web page.

Command-line scripts, however, produce text-only output, so you must use the newline character to format your output. If your script produces any output, you should always include \n after the last item has been displayed.

You can also take advantage of the fixed-width character mode when running command-line scripts—for instance, by spacing output into columns. The **printf** function allows you to use width and alignment format characters, which have no effect on HTML output unless they're contained in <PRE> tags. For more information, refer to Lesson 6, "Working with Strings."

Command-Line Arguments

You can pass arguments to a shell script by simply appending them after the script name itself. The number of arguments passed can be found in the variable $argc, and the arguments themselves are stored in a numerically indexed array named $argv.

> **Arguments** The identifier names argc and argv are
> used for historic reasons. They originated in C and are
> now widely used in many programming languages.
>
> In PHP $argc is assigned for convenience only; you
> could, of course, perform count($argv) to find out
> how many arguments were passed to the script.

The $argv array will always contain at least one element. Even if no additional arguments are passed to the script, $argv[0] will contain the name of the script itself, and $argc will be 1.

The script in Listing 21.1 requires exactly two arguments to be passed. Otherwise, an error message appears, and the script terminates. The output produced shows which of the two arguments is greater.

LISTING 21.1   Using Command-Line Arguments

```
#!/usr/local/bin/php
<?php

if ($argc != 3) {
  echo $argv[0].": Must provide exactly two arguments\n";
  exit;
}

if ($argv[1] < $argv[2]) {
  echo $argv[1] . " is less than ". $argv[2] . "\n";
}
elseif ($argv[1] > $argv[2]) {
  echo $argv[1] . " is greater than ". $argv[2] . "\n";
}
else {
  echo $argv[1] . " is equal to ". $argv[2] . "\n";
}
?>
```

Notice that the initial condition in Listing 21.1 checks that the value of $argc is 3; there must be two arguments, plus the script name itself in $argv[0]. In fact, $argv[0] is output as part of the error message. This is a useful technique for ensuring that the actual script name is shown, whatever its name happens to be.

Input/Output Streams

Although it is possible to read and write directly to the standard input, output, and error streams in the web environment, doing so is much more useful in command-line scripts.

Stream access is performed using the same set of functions as for file access: You simply open a file pointer to the appropriate stream and manipulate it in the same way.

The stream identifiers look like URLs—remember that PHP also allows you to open URLs by using the file access functions—constructed of php:// followed by the name of the stream. For instance, to open the standard input stream for reading, you use the following command:

```
$fp = fopen("php://stdin", "r");
```

However, because stream access is common in command-line scripts, PHP provides a shortcut. The constants STDIN, STDOUT, and STDERR provide instant access to an opened stream without requiring a call to fopen.

The script in Listing 21.2 uses all three standard streams. It reads data from standard input and capitalizes the letters it contains by using strtoupper. If the input data contains non-alphanumeric characters, a warning is sent to the standard error stream as well.

LISTING 21.2 Reading and Writing Standard Streams

```
#!/usr/local/bin/php
<?php

while (!feof(STDIN)) {
  $line++;
  $data = trim(fgets(STDIN));

  fputs(STDOUT, strtoupper($data)."\n");
  if (!ereg("^[[:alnum:]]+$", $data)) {
    fputs(STDERR,
        "Warning: Invalid characters on line $line\n");
  }
}
?>
```

If you run this script from the command line, it waits for you to type data a line at a time, and it returns the uppercase version after each line is entered. The advantage of using the standard input stream is that you can redirect input from another source.

To pass the contents of the file `myfile` into a script named `myscript` and have the output written to `outfile`, for instance, you would run the following command:

```
$ myscript < myfile > outfile
```

With the example in Listing 21.2, `outfile` would contain only the uppercase data. The warning messages produced would continue to be displayed to screen, unless you also redirected standard error.

To summarize, the constants and stream identifiers available in command-line PHP are shown in Table 21.1.

TABLE 21.1   Stream Access for CLI PHP

Constant	Identifier	Stream
STDIN	php://stdin	Standard input
STDOUT	php://stdout	Standard output
STDERR	php://stderr	Standard error

Creating Desktop Applications

PHP is such a powerful language that you can even use it to create desktop applications. Furthermore, because PHP is an interpreted language, any such applications are likely to be highly portable.

The PHP-GTK extension implements an interface to the GIMP window toolkit, GTK+. This provides PHP developers with the ability to create applications with a graphical front end that includes windows, menus, buttons, and even drag-and-drop functionality.

Creating a complex graphical application is beyond the scope of this book. If you are interested in learning more about PHP-GTK, however, see http://gtk.php.net.

Summary

In this lesson you have learned how to write PHP scripts by using the CLI. In the next lesson you will learn techniques for error handling and debugging in PHP.

LESSON 22
Error Handling

In this lesson you will learn how to deal with errors in PHP scripts effectively and how to debug code that does not work as you expect them to.

Error Reporting

PHP has a configurable error reporting system that you can set to be just as pedantic you want it to be about code. By default, the strictest mode is not enabled, and, in most cases, you get a warning message only when an imperfection has a good chance of affecting the intended purpose of your script.

Changing Error Levels

To change the error reporting level, you use the `error_reporting` function with a value that is made up of the constants shown in Table 22.1.

TABLE 22.1 Error Reporting Constants

Constant	Description
E_ERROR	Indicates a fatal runtime error. Script execution is halted.
E_WARNING	Issues runtime warnings. Non-fatal; script execution continues.
E_PARSE	Indicates compile-time parsing errors.
E_NOTICE	Issues runtime notices, which may or not indicate errors.

Constant	Description
E_CORE_ERROR	Issues a fatal error generated internally by PHP.
E_CORE_WARNING	Issues a warning generated internally by PHP.
E_COMPILE_ERROR	Issues a fatal error generated by the Zend engine.
E_COMPILE_WARNING	Issues a warning generated by the Zend engine.
E_USER_ERROR	Issues a user-generated error message, triggered by trigger_error.
E_USER_WARNING	Issues a user-generated warning, triggered by trigger_error.
E_USER_NOTICE	Issues a user-generated notice, triggered by trigger_error.
E_ALL	Issues all errors and warnings except E_STRICT.
E_STRICT	Issues all errors and warnings, plus PHP suggests code changes to improve code compatibility.

You combine these constants by using bitwise operators to create a bit-mask that represents the desired level. The default value is E_ALL & ~E_NOTICE, which means that all errors and warnings are displayed except for E_STRICT, which is not covered by E_ALL, and E_NOTICE.

To set the error reporting level so that all warnings and notices are displayed, you use the following command:

```
error_reporting(E_ALL);
```

The type of notices that are not displayed by default are not life-threatening and do not affect the normal execution of a script.

The E_NOTICE error level can be very useful during script development because it alerts you to the use of undefined variables. Although using E_NOTICE does not cause an error in your script, seeing these warnings can often alert you to an identifier name that was mistyped and should be referencing a previously declared value.

When you use E_NOTICE, you are also warned about certain points of coding style. For instance, array key identifiers should be enclosed in quotation marks, but a sloppy programmer might use $array[key]. PHP first assumes that key is a constant, but if no constant with that name is defined, it also tries to use it as a string key name. With E_NOTICE enabled, you are advised of this ambiguity.

The E_STRICT level is new in PHP 5, and it is useful if you want to make sure your code is up-to-date. It warns you if you use deprecated functions that have been left in the PHP language for backward compatibility.

You can also set the error reporting level in the php.ini file, or per directory, by using .htaccess, using the error_reporting directive. Lesson 23, "PHP Configuration," describes how to use these features.

> **Displaying Errors**   The log_errors and display_errors configuration directives allow you to choose whether errors and warnings are displayed to screen or written to a log file.
>
> On a production web site, you should consider whether displaying error messages onscreen is a security risk because it could convey information about your system to an intruder or a competitor.

Custom Error Handlers

PHP allows you to define a custom function that is called whenever an error is encountered. This replaces the default action of displaying the error message to screen or logging to a file, depending on your configuration.

You use the `set_error_handler` function to declare which function should be used as the custom error handler. Its first argument is the function name, and you can give an optional second argument that contains a bitmask that specifies which error levels should be handled by that function.

For example, to use the function `myhandler` to trap all `E_WARNING` and `E_NOTICE` errors, you use the following command:

```
set_error_handler("myhandler", E_WARNING & E_NOTICE);
```

The user-defined error handler function requires two parameters: an error code number and a string error message. The error code value can be compared to the constants in Table 22.1 to find out what type of error occurred. You can include three more optional parameters if you want to process the information they pass to the function: the filename, line number, and context when the error occurred.

The example in Listing 22.1 declares a custom error handler function that logs all errors to a MySQL database table.

LISTING 22.1   Writing a Custom Error Handler

```php
<?php

function log_errors($errno, $errstr, $errfile, $errline) {

    $db = mysql_connect("localhost", "loguser", "logpassword");
    mysql_select_db("test", $db);
    $errstr = mysql_escape_string($errstr);
    $sql = "insert into php_log
                (errno, errstr, errfile, errline)
            values
                ('$errno', '$errstr', '$errfile', '$errline')";

    $res = mysql_query($sql, $db);
}

set_error_handler("log_errors");

// Assigning an undefined variable will raise a warning
$a = $b;
?>
```

You create the database table required to log these errors by using the following SQL statement:

```
CREATE TABLE php_log (
  error_timestamp timestamp,
  errno int,
  errstr text,
  errfile text,
  errline int
);
```

Note that this example does not use the optional fifth parameter that passes in the context. The context is passed as an array that contains the contents of every variable—both local values and system super-globals—in the script at the time the error occurred.

Although this information can sometimes be useful when you're debugging, it is a lot of information to store to a log file or table. Furthermore, because the value passed is an array, you need to pass $errcontext through the serialize function in order to store it to a database or text file.

> **Context Data**   Most likely you are interested in only a small part of the context data passed to your error handler function, so you can have the function extract as much information as is necessary and discard the rest.

Raising User Errors

You can use the trigger_error function to raise an error on demand. If a custom error handler has been defined, it handles this user error. Otherwise, the default PHP error handler takes the appropriate action.

You should pass an error message string to the trigger_error function, and you can optionally give an error type constant. If no error type is given, E_USER_NOTICE is used.

For example, to raise a user notice type, you use this statement:

```
trigger_error("Some kind of error happened");
```

The error message displayed will look similar to the following:

```
Notice: Some kind of error happened in /home/chris/error.php
on line 3
```

To raise an error with the same message text but as a fatal error, you use this statement instead:

```
trigger_error("Some kind of error happened", E_USER_ERROR);
```

> **Error Types** You have to use the E_USER_ERROR and
> E_USER_WARNING types, not E_ERROR and E_WARNING, for
> user errors. An E_USER_ERROR type error is still treated
> as a fatal error, however, and script execution ends
> immediately when it occurs.

Logging Errors

You can accomplish most simple error logging requirements by using the error_log function. You can use this function to write an error message to the web server log file or some other local file, send it via email, or transmit it to a remote debugging service.

The error_log function takes the following arguments.

```
error_log($message, $message_type, $destination,
          $extra_headers);
```

Only the message argument is required, and the default action is to write this message text to the usual PHP log file. In most cases, this is your web server's log file.

The message_type argument specifies a number that determines what type of destination is supplied. Its possible values are shown in Table 22.2.

TABLE 22.2   `message_type` Argument Values in `error_log`

Value	Description
0	The message will be written to the default web server log file.
1	The message will be sent via email; `destination` contains the address to send to, and `extra_headers` contains optional email headers.
2	The message will be sent to a remote debugging service; `destination` contains the remote hostname. Note that remote debugging is not available in PHP 4 and later.
3	The message will be appended to a local file; `destination` contains the filename and path.

For example, to send an error message via email, you might use the following statement:

```
error_log("An error occurred in your script", 1,
          "chris@lightwood.net",
          "From: PHP Script Error <errors@yoursite.com>");
```

Suppressing Errors and Warnings

PHP allows you to suppress warning messages in your script. You can either turn off warnings completely or select individual commands for which any errors will not be displayed.

The Error Suppression Operator

If you want to stop a warning message from appearing for a particular statement only, you can use the @ symbol to silence it. You might want to do this so that your custom error messages are displayed.

For example, when you connect to a MySQL database, PHP raises its own error if the connection fails. You can also detect the failure by checking whether a valid database resource handle was returned. The following code uses the @ symbol to suppress the PHP error message so that only your message is displayed onscreen:

```
$db = @ mysql_connect("localhost", "username", "password");
if (!$db) {
  echo "Database connection failed";
  exit;
}
```

You can place the @ symbol before any expression in PHP. It causes any error messages generated as a result of that expression being evaluated to be ignored.

In the preceding example, the expression being silenced is the database connection attempt. As a general rule, if something in PHP has a value, it can be prefixed with the @ symbol. You cannot prepend an @ symbol to a language construct such as a function definition or conditional statement.

> **Parsing Errors**   The @ operator does not hide error messages caused by parsing errors in script.

The following statement is also valid, although it does not make it clear that you are expecting the error message to originate with mysql_connect:

```
@ $db = mysql_connect("localhost", "username", "password");
```

> **Error Suppression**   If you have used set_error_ handler to specify a custom error handler in your script, the @ operator will have no effect.

Preventing Error Display

The configuration directive display_errors can be set to Off in php.ini to prevent any errors from being displayed onscreen. You will learn how to change the value of php.ini settings in Lesson 23.

If you choose to prevent error display for your whole website this way, you should turn on the `log_errors` setting so that errors and warnings are written to a file; otherwise, you will have no way of knowing about potential problems. You should not consider turning `display_errors` off while a website is in development.

Summary

In this lesson you have learned how to detect and handle errors in PHP scripts. In the next lesson you will learn about the various PHP settings that you can configure to suit your particular needs.

LESSON 23
PHP Configuration

In this lesson you will learn how to configure global PHP settings at run-time, using the php.ini *file, and per-directory settings, using* .htaccess.

Configuration Settings

PHP allows you to tune many aspects of its behavior by using a set of configuration directives. These directives can be global for your entire web server, or you can make local changes that apply only to certain scripts.

Using php.ini

PHP's configuration file is named php.ini. Its location is set at compile time; by default, it is located in /usr/local/lib/php.ini on Linux/Unix servers and C:\WINDOWS\php.ini on Windows systems.

The php.ini file contains a list of configuration directives and their values, separated by equals signs. The default php.ini file distributed with PHP is well documented, with plenty of comments. Any line that begins with a semicolon is considered a comment, and sections of the file are broken up using headings in square brackets, which the compiler also ignores.

Listing 23.1 shows an extract from an unchanged php.ini file for PHP 5 that contains the log settings. As you can see, for many setting changes, you do not even need to refer to the online documentation.

LISTING 23.1   An Extract from `php.ini`

```
; Print out errors (as a part of the output).  For
; production web sites,
; you're strongly encouraged to turn this feature off,
; and use error logging
; instead (see below).  Keeping display_errors enabled
; on a production web site
; may reveal security information to end users, such as
; file paths on your Web
; server, your database schema or other information.
display_errors = On

; Even when display_errors is on, errors that occur
; during PHP's startup
; sequence are not displayed.  It's strongly recommended
; to keep
; display_startup_errors off, except for when debugging.
display_startup_errors = Off

; Log errors into a log file (server-specific log, stderr,
; or error_log (below))
; As stated above, you're strongly advised to use error
; logging in place of
; error displaying on production web sites.
log_errors = Off

; Set maximum length of log_errors. In error_log information
; about the source is
; added. The default is 1024 and 0 allows to not apply any
;maximum length at all
.
log_errors_max_len = 1024
```

> **True or False**   Boolean values in `php.ini` can be set to
> `true` (that is, `on` or `yes`) or `false` (that is, `off`, `no`, or
> `none`). These values are not case-sensitive.

When it runs as a web server module, `php.ini` is read when the web
server process starts, and changes made to the configuration file do not
take place until the web server is restarted.

If your web server runs PHP as a CGI binary, the php.ini settings are loaded each time a script is run because a new php process is started. Similarly, command-line PHP loads the settings from php.ini each time a script is run.

Alternate php.ini Files

You can create separate php.ini files to apply for the different ways PHP can be run. If you create a file named php-SAPI.ini (replacing SAPI with the a valid SAPI name), that file is read instead of the global php.ini.

For instance, to provide a different set of directives only for command-line PHP, you would use a configuration file named php-cli.ini. For the Apache web server module, the filename would be php-apache.ini.

On a Windows system, a php.ini file in the Apache installation directory is used before one in C:\WINDOWS. This allows you to maintain different PHP settings for multiple web servers on the same machine.

To force the use of a particular configuration file, you must invoke php with the -c option. In a shell script, you might change the first line to the following to force a custom configuration file to be used only for that script:

```
#!/usr/local/bin/php -c /path/to/php.ini
```

Per-Directory Configuration

Apache web server allows you to use a per-directory configuration file named .htaccess to supply custom web server directives. PHP supports the use of .htaccess to override the global settings from php.ini.

To give a new value for a PHP setting, you use php_value followed by the directive from php.ini and the new value. The following line in an .htaccess file gives a new value for max_execution_time of 60 seconds:

```
php_value max_execution_time 60
```

> **Using .htaccess** Be aware of the syntax difference
> when changing configuration settings in php.ini and
> .htaccess. In php.ini there must be an equals sign
> between the directive name and the value. In
> .htaccess the value follows the directive name, with
> no equals sign.

Changes made in .htaccess apply only to the directory in which it
resides and its subdirectories. Any settings in .htaccess override the
global php.ini as well as any settings made in an .htaccess file in a parent directory.

Dynamic Configuration

You can alter values of directives set in php.ini on-the-fly by using the
ini_set function. It takes two arguments: the directive name and the new
value. When you change a setting by using ini_set, the return value is
the previous setting for that directive.

The following example changes the memory_limit setting for the current
script to run a section of code that may require more resources than usual:

```
$limit = ini_set("memory_limit", "128M");
// Execute code that requires this setting
ini_set("memory_limit", $limit);
```

The previous value is saved to a variable and then restored when the
intensive code has completed.

To find the current value of any php.ini setting without changing it, you
use the ini_get function.

Configuration Directives

This lesson cannot cover every configuration directive in php.ini in
detail—there are simply too many. However, in the following sections you
will learn how some of the most commonly used settings work. For a full
reference, refer to www.php.net/manual/en/ini.php.

Configuring the PHP Environment

The following sections list some of the common configuration directives that affect the environment in which PHP runs. Each directive listed in the following sections is shown with its default entry from the php.ini file that is distributed with PHP 5, where the default is set.

PHP Tag Styles

These directives allow you to select which tag styles can be used in a PHP script:

- **short_open_tag = On**—The short_open_tag directive enables or disables the use of the <? opening tag. If this setting is turned off, your scripts must use the full <?php tag.

  Because <? can have other meanings when embedded in a web page, you should try to avoid using short_open_tag, and in future releases of PHP, it may be disabled by default.

- **asp_tags = Off**—The asp_tags style of PHP tag begins with <% and ends with %>. You must enable this style in php.ini if you want to use it.

System Resource Limits

The following directives allow you to manage the system resources available to a PHP script:

- **max_execution_time = 30;**—The max_execution_time directive specifies the maximum total number of seconds that a script can run. After this time is exceeded, an error occurs, and script execution stops.

  Unless you have a specific need for a higher value in order to run slow scripts, you should not change this value. An accidental infinite loop in your script would eat up a lot of system resources, and max_execution_time is a safeguard against this kind of problem.

  If a web page takes 30 seconds or more to load, visitors will probably not wait for it to finish, unless they have requested some specific information that they understand may take some time to generate.

- `memory_limit = 8M`—Each PHP script has a memory usage limit to make sure that the work it is doing does not get out of control and affect the system in a negative way. Most scripts use only a very small amount of memory; to find out just how much, you can call the `memory_get_usage` function.

  The `M` suffix indicates a value in megabytes; the `K` or `G` suffix could also be used, to indicate kilobytes or gigabytes, respectively. If you are absolutely sure you want to remove the memory limit completely, you can set `memory_limit` to `-1`.

Form Processing

You can use these directives to change the way PHP interacts with web forms:

- `magic_quotes`—The `magic_quotes` settings instruct PHP to automatically delimit quotes so that they are safe to use as string values. These are the defaults:

```
magic_quotes_gpc = On
magic_quotes_runtime = Off
magic_quotes_sybase = Off
```

  The `magic_quotes_gpc` setting applies to data posted from a form and data from cookie values. (gpc stands for GET, POST, and COOKIE data.) The `magic_quotes_runtime` directive tells PHP to delimit quotes in data generated by the script, such as from a database query or host command.

  Usually, quotes are delimited with a backslash character, but some databases, notably Sybase, use another quote character. When the `magic_quotes_sybase` setting is enabled, delimited quotes appear as `' '` instead of `\ '`.

- `register_globals = Off`—The `register_globals` setting has been disabled in PHP by default since version 4.2. When it is enabled, this option causes PHP to create global variables that contain the same information as the super-globals $_ENV, $_GET, $_POST, $_COOKIE, and $_SERVER. The variable names correspond to the key names in each of the super-global arrays.

- **variables_order = "EGPCS"**—The variables_order directive determines the order in which global variables are registered from the super-globals. With register_globals enabled and the default ordering, a cookie named email is registered more recently than a posted form value with the same name, so $email in the script contains the cookie's value.

  Because register_globals creates values that are not distinguished by their source, it is strongly recommended that you use the super-global arrays; when you do so, you can be confident that $_POST["email"] was a form-submitted value, but $email could have come from one of several sources.

- **register_long_arrays = On**—Older PHP versions use arrays named $HTTP_GET_VARS, $HTTP_POST_VARS, $HTTP_SERVER_VARS, and so on instead of the newer super-global arrays. The register_long_arrays directive determines whether arrays with these names are created. This feature remains enabled by default for backward compatibility.

Include Files

You can use the include_path directive to give a list of locations in which to search for a file referenced in an include or require statement. The locations are separated by colons on Linux/Unix systems and by semicolons on Windows systems.

Often you need to ensure that include files are kept in a directory that is not directly accessible by a web server. The following example defines an include path that contains a directory parallel to the web root of /home/chris/public_html:

```
php_value include_path .:/home/chris/include
```

The period character (.) is used to indicate the current working directory, and in this example, it is given higher priority than the defined include directory. In this case, if an `include` statement finds a matching file in both locations, the one in the working directory will be used. This type of configuration allows you to use shared library files across your server but override them for some scripts when necessary.

The `auto_prepend_file` and `auto_append_file` directives allow you to specify files that are automatically added at the start and end of each PHP script. The filename given is found in `include_path`, or a full path to the file can be given.

A common use for `auto_prepend_file` is to automatically include part of the HTML layout before the output from your script so that all your pages look the same. Because `auto_prepend_file` is a PHP feature, only files parsed by PHP have the file prepended; static HTML pages do not.

> **HTTP Headers**   After any output has been sent to the browser, you cannot use the `header` function to send HTTP headers or use any other PHP functions that require headers to be sent, such as session control functions or cookies. Therefore, any script included by `auto_prepend_file` must produce no output if you want to send custom HTTP headers.

Error Logging

As you learned in Lesson 22, "Error Handling," PHP allows you to configure the strictness of error reporting and the means by which it is reported.

The value of the `error_reporting` directive is a bitmask comprised of the values found in Table 22.1 in Lesson 22. You can use logical operators to combine values as follows:

```
error_reporting  =  E_ALL & ~E_NOTICE & ~E_STRICT
```

The `display_errors` and `log_errors` directives determine whether an error is written to the screen display and web server log file, respectively.

The default settings are as follows, with errors displayed to screen and not written to a file:

```
display_errors = On
log_errors = Off
```

You can use the `error_log` directive to specify an alternate filename, as in the following example:

```
error_log = /tmp/php_log
```

Configuring PHP Extensions

Some PHP extensions have their own directives that can be configured in `php.ini` to adjust the behavior of that extension.

For clarity in the configuration file, section headings are used to separate extension-specific settings. For instance, all the settings that affect the MySQL extension are found in a section of `php.ini` that begins `[MySQL]`. Each directive name also has a prefix that indicates the extension to which it belongs (for example, `mysql.connect_timeout` or `session.cookie_path`).

You can find documentation for extension-specific configuration directives in the online manual pages for each extension.

Configuring System Security

Some of the directives in `php.ini` that are not covered in this lesson—most notably the `safe_mode` directive and its related settings—concern server security. These configuration options allow you to restrict certain types of functionality on the web server, and you will learn about them in Lesson 24, "PHP Security."

Loadable Modules

PHP allows you to load certain extensions at runtime. This means that you can extend the functionality of PHP without needing to recompile from source.

Loading Extensions on Demand

You use the `dl` function to dynamically load an extension module. You build extensions as dynamically loadable objects when PHP is compiled, by using the `--with-EXTENSION=shared` switch. For instance, running the following `configure` statement causes PHP to be compiled with MySQL support linked in but with socket support as a loadable extension:

```
./configure --with-mysql --with-sockets=shared
```

The argument given to `dl` is the filename of the extension. In the case of the sockets extension, it would be called `sockets.so` on Linux/Unix but `php_sockets.dll` on Windows systems.

> **Loadable Extensions**   Whether the `dl` function is available is governed by the `enable_dl` directive in `php.ini`. You may find that on a shared web hosting service, this feature is not available to you.

To check whether an extension is loaded into PHP, you use the `extension_loaded` function. Given an extension name argument, this function returns TRUE or FALSE, depending on the presence of that extension. Note that PHP cannot tell whether an extension was loaded by using `dl` or is compiled in.

Loading Modules on Startup

If you have extensions as loadable modules and want them to be loaded into PHP without needing to run `dl` in every script, you can use the `extension` directive in `php.ini` to provide a list of extensions to load at startup.

Each extension is given on a separate line, and there is no limit to the number of extensions you can load in this way. The following lines from php.ini ensure that the sockets and imap extensions are loaded automatically on a Linux/Unix server:

```
extension=imap.so
extension=sockets.so
```

On a Windows web server, the configuration lines need to look like this, to reflect the difference in filenames between the two platforms:

```
extension=php_imap.dll
extension=php_sockets.dll
```

Summary

In this lesson you have learned how to configure PHP at runtime. In the next lesson you will learn about PHP's Safe Mode and how to minimize security threats to your website.

LESSON 24
PHP Security

PHP is undoubtedly a very powerful server-side scripting language, but with great power comes great responsibility. In this lesson you will learn how to use PHP's Safe Mode to make sure that some of the potentially dangerous features of PHP are locked down.

Safe Mode

PHP's Safe Mode attempts to provide a degree of basic security in a shared environment, where multiple user accounts exist on a PHP-enabled web server.

When a web server is running PHP in Safe Mode, some functions are disabled completely, and others are available with limited functionality.

Restrictions Enforced by Safe Mode

Functions that attempt to access the filesystem have restricted functionality in Safe Mode. The web server process runs under the same user ID for all web space accounts and must have the appropriate read or write permission to access a file. This is a requirement of the underlying operating system and has nothing to do with PHP itself.

When Safe Mode is enabled and an attempt is made to read or write a local file, PHP checks whether file ownership of the script is the same as that of the target file. If the owner differs, the operation is prohibited.

The following core filesystem functions are restricted by this rule:

chdir	move_uploaded_file
chgrp	parse_ini_file
chown	rmdir
copy	rename
fopen	require
highlight_file	show_source
include	symlink
link	touch
mkdir	unlink

Functions that are part of PHP extensions that also access the filesystem are similarly affected.

Functions that execute host programs are disabled unless they are run from the directory given in the safe_mode_exec_dir directive, which you will learn about in the next section. Even if execution is allowed, arguments to the commands are automatically passed to the escapeshellcmd function.

The following program execution functions are affected by this rule:

exec	shell_exec
passthru	system
popen	

In addition, the backtick operator (`) is disabled.

The putenv function has no effect when run in Safe Mode, although no error is produced. Similarly, other functions that attempt to change the PHP environment, such as set_time_limit and set_include_path, are ignored.

Enabling Safe Mode

You turn Safe Mode on or off by using the safe_mode directive in php.ini. To activate Safe Mode for all users on a shared web server, you use the following directive:

```
safe_mode = On
```

As you learned in the previous section, functions that access the filesystem perform a check on the owner of the file. By default, the check is performed on the file owner's user ID, but you can relax this to check the owner's group ID (GID) instead by turning on the safe_mode_gid directive.

If you have shared library files on your system, you can use the safe_mode_include_dir directive to get a list of locations for which the UID/GID check will not be performed when an include or require statement is encountered.

Include Directories   If you want to list more than one location in the `safe_mode_include_dir` directive, you can separate them using colons on Linux/Unix or semicolons on Windows systems—just as you do with the `include_path` setting.

To allow inclusion of files in `/usr/local/include/php` for any user in Safe Mode, you would use the following directive:

```
safe_mode_include_dir = /usr/local/include/php
```

To provide a location from which the system can be executed, you use the `safe_mode_exec_dir` directive.

To allow programs in `/usr/local/php-bin` to be executed in Safe Mode, you would use the following directive:

```
safe_mode_exec_dir = /usr/local/php-bin
```

Executables   Rather than allow execution of all programs from `/usr/bin` or some other system location, you should create a new directory and copy or link only selected binaries into it.

To allow setting of certain environment variables, you use the `safe_mode_allowed_env_vars` directive. The value given is a prefix, and by default it allows only environment variables that begin with PHP_ to be changed. If more than one value is given, the list should be separated by commas.

The following directive also allows the time zone environment variable, TZ, to be changed:

```
safe_mode_allowed_env_vars = PHP_,TZ
```

Other Security Features

In addition to Safe Mode, PHP provides a number of functions that allow you to place restrictions on the features available to PHP.

Hiding PHP

You can use the expose_php directive in php.ini to prevent the presence of PHP being reported by the web server, as follows:

```
expose_php = On
```

By using this setting, you can discourage automated scripts from trying to attack your web server. Usually, the HTTP headers contain a line that looks like the following:

```
Server: Apache/1.3.33 (Unix) PHP/5.0.3 mod_ssl/2.8.16
OpenSSL/0.9.7c
```

With the expose_php directive enabled, the PHP version is not included in this header.

Of course, the .php file extension is a giveaway to visitors that PHP is in use on a website. If you want to use a totally different file extension, you need to first find the following line in httpd.conf:

```
AddType application/x-httpd .php
```

Then you need to change .php to any file extension you like. You can specify any number of file extensions, separated by spaces. To have PHP parse .html and .htm files so there is no indication that a server-side language is being used at all, you can use the following directive:

```
AddType application/x-httpd .html .htm
```

> **Parsing HTML**   Configuring your web server to parse
> all HTML files with PHP may be convenient, but a
> small performance hit is involved because the PHP
> parser needs to fire up even if there is no server-side
> code in a web page.
>
> By using a different file extension for static pages, you
> can eliminate the need for PHP to be involved where
> it is not necessary.

Filesystem Security

Safe Mode restricts filesystem access only to files owned by the script
owner, and you can use the open_basedir directive to specify the directory in which a file must reside. If you specify a directory, PHP will
refuse any attempt to access a file that is not in that directory or its subdirectory tree. The open_basedir directive works independently of Safe
Mode.

To restrict filesystem access on your web server to only the /tmp directory, you use the following directive:

```
open_basedir = /tmp
```

Function Access Control

You can use the disable_functions directive to specify a comma-
delimited list of function names that will be disabled in the PHP language.
This setting works independently of Safe Mode.

To disable the dl function without turning on Safe Mode, you use the following directive:

```
disable_functions = dl
```

You can also disable access to classes by using the disable_classes
directive in the same way.

Database Security

You learned in Lesson 18, "Host Program Execution," how a malicious user might try to run an arbitrary host command on your system, and that you can use the escapeshellcmd function to prevent this kind of abuse.

A similar situation applies to database use through PHP. Suppose your script contains the following lines to execute a MySQL query based on a form value:

```
$sql = "UPDATE mytable SET col1 = " . $_POST["value"] . "
        WHERE col2 = 'somevalue'";
$res = mysql_query($sql, $db);
```

You are expecting $_POST["value"] to contain an integer value to update the value of column col1. However, a malicious user could enter a semi-colon in the form input field, followed by any SQL statement he or she wants to execute.

For instance, suppose the following is the value of $_POST["value"]:

```
0; INSERT INTO admin_users (username, password)
VALUES ('me', 'mypassword');
```

The SQL executed would then look like the following (the statements are shown here on separate lines for clarity):

```
UPDATE mytable SET col1 = 0;
INSERT INTO admin_users (username, password)
VALUES ('me', 'mypassword');
WHERE col2 = 'somevalue';
```

This is clearly a bad situation! The first statement updates the value of col1 for all rows in mytable. This will be an inconvenience, but the second statement creates a more serious problem—the user has been able to execute an INSERT statement that creates a new administrator login. The third statement is rubbish, but by the time the SQL parser reaches that statement and throws an error, the damage has been done. This type of attack is known as *SQL injection*.

Of course, for SQL injection to be a serious threat, the user must understand a little about your database structure. In this example, the attacker is aware that you have a table called admin_users, that it contains fields named `username` and `password`, and that the password is stored unencrypted.

A visitor to your website would not generally know such information about a database you built yourself. However, if your website includes open-source components—perhaps you have used a freeware discussion board program—the table definitions for at least some of your database are accessible to users.

Furthermore, if your script produces output whenever a query fails, this could reveal important details about your database structure. On a production website, you should consider setting `display_errors` to `off` and using `log_errors` to write warnings and error messages to a file instead.

Database Permissions   It is vital that the database connection from your script be made by a database user who has only just enough access rights to perform the job.

You should certainly never connect as an administrator from a script. If you did, an attacker would be able to gain full access to your database and others on the same server. Attackers will also be able to run the `GRANT` or `CREATE USER` command to give themselves full access outside the confines of your script!

To prevent the possibility of a SQL injection attack, you must ensure that user-submitted data that forms part of a query cannot be used to interrupt the SQL statement that you intend to execute.

The previous example shows an integer value being updated. If this were a string value enclosed in single quotes, the attacker would need to submit a closing quote before the semicolon and then the SQL statement. However, when `magic_quotes_gpc` is turned on, a quotation mark submitted via a web form will be automatically delimited.

To be absolutely sure that form-submitted values are not vulnerable to SQL injection attacks, you should always ensure that the data received is appropriate. If your query expects a numeric value, you should test the form value with is_numeric or use settype to convert it to a number, removing any characters that are designed to fool SQL.

If you are working with several user-submitted values in one SQL statement, you can use the sprintf function to build a SQL statement string, using format characters that indicate the data type of each value. The following is an example:

```
$sql = sprintf("UPDATE mytable SET col1 = %d
               WHERE col2 = '%s'",
               $_POST["number"],
               mysql_escape_string($_POST["string"]));
```

The preceding example assumes that a MySQL database is being used, so the string value is passed to mysql_escape_string. For other databases, you should ensure that quote characters are adequately delimited, by using addslashes or another suitable method.

Summary

In this lesson you have learned about the security considerations involved in building a dynamic website using PHP. In the next lesson you will learn about PEAR—PHP's primary resource for third-party add-ons.

LESSON 25
Using PEAR

In this lesson you will learn about the PHP Extension and Application Repository (PEAR).

Introducing PEAR

PEAR is a framework and distribution system for reusable PHP packages. PEAR is made up of the following:

- A structured library of open-source code for PHP developers
- A system for distributing and maintaining code in packages
- The PEAR Coding Standards (PCS)
- The PHP Foundation Classes (PFC)
- Online support for the PEAR community through a website and mailing list

The PEAR Code Library

PEAR brings together many different open-source projects, each of which is bundled into its own package. Each PEAR package has its own maintainers and developers, who determine the changes and release cycle for their own packages, but the package structure is consistent for all PEAR projects.

You use the PEAR installer, which is shipped with PHP, to automatically download and install a PEAR package by simply giving its name. You will learn how to use the PEAR installer later in this lesson.

Each package may have dependencies from other PEAR packages, and this is explicitly noted in the documentation, even if packages appear to be related because of their names.

A package tree structure exists within PEAR, and an underscore character (_) separates nodes in the hierarchy. For instance, the HTTP package contains various HTTP utilities, whereas HTTP_Header deals specifically with HTTP header requests.

Package Distribution and Maintenance

PEAR packages are registered in a central database at http://pear.php.net. The PEAR website provides a searchable interface to the database by package name, category, and release date.

Maintainers of PEAR packages use the PEAR website to manage their projects. A CVS server allows developers to collaborate on source code and, once a release has been agreed upon, it can be made available from this central location immediately.

PEAR Coding Standards

The PCS documents were created because many different teams are developing open-source packages that might be of use to the PHP community.

The documents in PCS outline a structured way in which code should be written in order for a package to be accepted as part of the PEAR project. The standards are quite detailed and contain mostly points of style, such as identifier naming conventions and a consistent style to use when declaring functions and classes.

This may sound a little daunting, but as your scripts become more complicated, you will realize how important it is to write readable code, and you will begin to develop a clear coding style. The PCS documentation simply formalizes a set of guidelines for writing readable PHP.

You can find the PCS documents online at http://pear.php.net/manual/en/standards.php.

PHP Foundation Classes

PFC is a subset of PEAR packages, and these classes have a strict set of entrance criteria:

- **Quality**—Packages must be in a stable state.

- **Generality**—Packages should not be excessively specific to any particular type of environment.

- **Interoperability**—Packages should work well with other packages and in different environments, and they should have a standardized API.

- **Compatibility**—Packages must be designed to be backward compatible when new features are added.

At the present time, only the PEAR installer is shipped with PHP. However, at a later date, certain classes may be included as standard. The PFC would be those classes.

Online Support for PEAR

The PEAR website, at http://pear.php.net, includes comprehensive online documentation for the PEAR project. The package database can be searched via the website, and package maintainers can log in to update their project details.

There are a number of mailing lists for PEAR users, maintainers, core developers, and webmasters. You can join any or all of these lists by using the form at http://pear.php.net/support/lists.php.

Using PEAR

In the following sections you will learn how to use PEAR to find and install packages on a system, and you'll learn how to submit your own projects for consideration as PEAR packages.

Finding a PEAR Package

On every page of the PEAR website is a search box that you can use to search the package database. You simply enter a name, or part of a name, and all matching packages are displayed.

> 💡 **Searching Packages**   To perform a detailed search
> on a package name, maintainer, or release date,
> you can use the form at http://pear.php.net/
> package-search.php.

You can click the name of the package you are interested in from the search results. The page that is then displayed should give some key information about that package, including a summary of its features, the current release version, and status and information about its dependencies—that is, any other PEAR packages that are required for this package to work.

The tabs at the top of the package details page allow you to view the documentation. If you are unsure from the summary information about exactly what you can achieve by using a particular package, you can browse through the documentation pages.

If you simply want to browse all the available PEAR packages, you can go to the categorized list at http://pear.php.net/packages.php.

Using the PEAR Installer

When you have decided that a package will be useful, you can download it from the web by using the tab at the top of its package information page. However, using the PEAR installer program is a quick and easy way to manage packages within a PHP installation. The installer is able to find and download the latest version of a package and can also install it for you automatically.

The PEAR installer is named `pear`. To run the installer, you run the `pear` command followed by a command option. To see all the packages currently installed on a system, you can use the `list` command option:

```
$ pear list
```

> **Command Options**   Running pear with no arguments
> brings up a list of all the available command options.

The output produced should be similar to the following:

```
Installed packages:
====================
Package        Version State
DB             1.6.2   stable
HTTP           1.2.2   stable
Net_DNS        1.00b2  beta
Net_SMTP       1.2.6   stable
Net_Socket     1.0.1   stable
PEAR           1.3.2   stable
SQLite         1.0.2   stable
```

Each package name, the version installed, and its release status are shown. The actual packages installed on your system may differ from the ones shown here.

You can use the search command option to search the PEAR package database. To search for all packages that contain the string mail, you run the following command:

```
# pear search mail
```

The output produced displays all matching packages, their latest version numbers, and a brief summary. The search performed is not case-sensitive.

To view all the available stable PEAR packages, you use the list-all command:

```
# pear list-all
```

This produces a long list!

To download and install a package, you use the install command option followed by the name of the package. To install the Mail package, you issue the following command:

```
# pear install Mail_Queue
```

Some packages cannot be installed unless others are already installed on your system, and installation will fail if the required packages are not found. The following output shows an attempt to install the `Mail_Queue` package before the `Mail` package has been installed:

```
# pear install Mail_Queue
downloading Mail_Queue-1.1.3.tar ...
Starting to download Mail_Queue-1.1.3.tar (-1 bytes)
.....done: 98,816 bytes
requires package `Mail'
Mail_Queue: Dependencies failed
```

Some dependencies are optional. When you install the `Mail` package to fix the dependency reported in the previous error message, PEAR advises you that the functionality of the `Mail` package can be enhanced if you also install `Net_SMTP`:

```
# pear install Mail
downloading Mail-1.1.4.tar ...
Starting to download Mail-1.1.4.tar (-1 bytes)
.....done: 73,728 bytes
Optional dependencies:
package `Net_SMTP' version >= 1.1.0 is recommended to
utilize some features.
install ok: Mail 1.1.4
```

You can use the `upgrade` command option to download and install a later version of an installed package. To check whether a new version of the `Mail` package is released, you use the following command:

```
# pear upgrade Mail
```

If a later version than the one installed is found, it is upgraded automatically.

> **Upgrading Packages**   You can use the `upgrade-all` command to check for newer versions of all your installed PEAR packages at once.

If you want to remove a PEAR package completely, you use the `uninstall` command.

Contributing Your Own PEAR Project

If you have written a PHP project that you think will be useful to other developers, you might consider submitting a proposal to have it included in PEAR.

The online documentation (at http://pear.php.net/manual/en/ guide-newmaint.php) includes a guide for project maintainers that details the process of first making sure that your project is suitable for submission to PEAR and then ensuring that your code is of a suitable standard. You should read that guide if you intend to write a package suitable for use by other developers. Even if your project is not suitable for PEAR, these guidelines will make you think about your software design and coding standards and will help you produce a much higher-quality package.

Summary

In this lesson you have learned how to use PEAR. Now that you have completed this book, you can take advantage of the many freely available PEAR classes so that you can create PHP scripts that perform a wide variety of functions. Happy coding!

APPENDIX A
Installing PHP

If you need to install PHP for yourself, this appendix is for you: It takes you through the process step-by-step, on both Linux/Unix and Windows platforms.

Linux/Unix Installation

These instructions take you through installing PHP from source, using an Apache web server. You should become the root user to perform the installation by issuing the su command and entering the superuser password.

Compiling Apache from Source

If you already have installed an Apache web server that supports dynamic shared objects (DSO), you can skip this section. To check whether your web server includes this feature, run the following command:

```
$ httpd -l
```

If the output includes mod_so.c, then DSO support is included. Note that you may have to supply the full path to httpd (for instance, /usr/local/apache/bin/httpd).

You begin by downloading the latest Apache source code from http://httpd.apache.org. At the time of this writing, the latest version is 2.0.52, so the file to download is called httpd-2.0.52.tar.bz2. If a later version is available, you should be sure to substitute the appropriate version number wherever it appears in a filename.

You need to save this file to your filesystem in /usr/local/src or some other place where you keep source code. Uncompress the archive using bunzip2, as follows:

```
# bunzip2 httpd-2.0.52.tar.bz2
```

When the file has been uncompressed, it loses the `.bz2` file extension. You extract this archive file by using `tar`:

```
# tar xvf httpd-2.0.52.tar
```

Files are extracted to a directory called `httpd-2.0.52`. You should change to this new directory before continuing:

```
# cd httpd-2.0.52
```

Next, you should issue the `configure` command with any configuration switches that are appropriate. For instance, to change the base installation directory, you should use the `--prefix` switch, followed by the desired location. You can enter `configure --help` to see a list of the possible configure switches.

You need to include at least the `--enable-module=so` switch to ensure that DSO support is available for loading the PHP module later on. You should enter the following command, adding any other configuration switches that you need to include:

```
# ./configure --enable-module=so
```

The `configure` command produces several screens full of output as it tries to detect the best compilation settings for your system. When it is done, you are returned to a shell prompt and can continue the installation.

To begin compiling, you issue the `make` command:

```
# make
```

Again, a lot of output is produced, and the time required for compilation depends on the speed of your system. When the build is done, you see the following line and are returned to a shell prompt:

```
make[1]: Leaving directory `/usr/local/src/httpd-2.0.52'
```

The final step is to install the newly built software. To do this, you simply enter `make install`, and the files are automatically copied to their correct system locations:

```
# make install
```

You issue the apachectl start command to start the Apache web server and enter your server's IP address in a web browser to test that the installation is successful. You use the following command if you have not changed the default installation location:

```
# /usr/local/apache/bin/apachectl start
```

Compiling and Installing PHP

You can download the latest version of PHP from www.php.net/downloads.php. At the time of this writing, the latest version is 5.0.3, so the file to download is called php-5.0.3.tar.bz2. If a later version is available, you should be sure to substitute the appropriate version number wherever it appears in a filename.

You need to save this file to your filesystem in /usr/local/src or some other place where you keep source code. You uncompress the archive by using bunzip2, as follows:

```
# bunzip2 php-5.0.3.tar.bz2
```

Uncompressing   If your system does not include the bunzip2 utility, you should download the file called httpd-2.0.52.tar.gz instead. This archive is slightly larger but is compressed using gzip, which is more widely available.

When the file has been uncompressed, it loses the .bz2 file extension. Extract this uncompressed archive file by using tar:

```
# tar xvf php-5.0.3.tar
```

Files are extracted to a directory called php-5.0.3. You should change to this new directory before continuing:

```
# cd php-5.0.3
```

Next, you should issue the configure command with any configuration switches that are appropriate. For example, to include database support through the MySQLi extension, you would use the --with-mysqli switch, followed by the path to the mysql_config utility. To see the full list of configure switches, you can run configure --help.

You need to include either the --with-apxs or --with-apxs2 switch—the latter is for Apache 2.0—followed by the location of the apxs utility on your system. You would use one of the following statements with a default Apache installation:

```
# ./configure --with-apxs2=/usr/local/apache2/bin/apxs

# ./configure --with-apxs2=/usr/local/apache/bin/apxs
```

The configure command produces several screens full of output as it tries to detect the best compilation settings for your system. When it is done, you are returned to a shell prompt and can continue the installation.

To begin compiling, you issue the make command:

```
# make
```

Again, a lot of output is produced, and the time required for compilation depends on the speed of your system. When the build is done, you see the following text and are returned to a shell prompt:

```
Build complete.
(It is safe to ignore warnings about tempnam and tmpnam).
```

The final step is to install the newly built PHP module into your web server. To do this, you enter make install, and the files are automatically copied to their correct system locations:

```
# make install
```

To complete the installation, you need to make a change to the web server configuration file to tell it that .php files should be passed to the PHP module. You should edit the httpd.conf file to add the following line:

```
AddType application/x-httpd-php .php
```

You can include other file extensions besides .php if you want.

When you next restart your web server by using the apachectl restart command, the PHP extension will be loaded. To test PHP, you can create a simple script, `/usr/local/apache2/htdocs/index.php`, that looks like this:

```
<?php
phpinfo();
?>
```

In your web browser, you can visit `index.php` on the IP address of your web server, and you should see a page that gives lots of information about the PHP configuration.

Windows Installation

The instructions in this section take you through installing PHP into an Apache web server on a Windows system.

Installing Apache

If you already have an Apache web server installed on your system, you can skip this section.

Download the latest version of Apache from `httpd.apache.org`. The file to get is the MSI Installer package, named `apache_2.0.52-win32-x86-no_ssl.msi` for the current Apache 2.0.52 release. Save this file to your desktop and double-click to begin the installation process.

The installation process is done through a wizard and is mostly self-explanatory. You must accept the license terms to continue with the installation, after which you are shown some release notes. Click Next after you have read these, and you are asked to enter your server information.

Enter your server's domain name and hostname and your email address. If you are installing on a personal workstation, you should use `localhost` and `localdomain` for your server information. You should leave the recommended option to install Apache on port 80 selected.

When asked to choose a setup type, you should select the typical setup. Then you are given the opportunity to select the destination folder for the Apache files. By default, this is `C:\Program Files\Apache Group`. Finally, Apache is ready to install, and clicking the Install button causes your system to start copying and setting up files on your system.

When the installation is complete, the Apache server and monitor program start up, and you see a new icon in your system tray. You can double-click this icon to bring up the Apache Service Monitor, which you can use to start and stop the web server process. A green light indicates a running server.

Installing PHP

You can download the latest version of PHP from the Windows Binaries section of www.php.net/downloads.php. You should choose the zip file rather than the installer package; it is named php-5.0.3-Win32.zip for the latest version of PHP, which is 5.0.3 at this writing. If a later version is available, be sure to substitute the appropriate version number wherever it appears in a filename.

You need to save the zip file to your desktop and double-click it to extract it to C:\php. You can choose another location, as long as you also change the other instructions in this section to reflect it.

Next, you need to add the PHP module to Apache. Using the file explorer, you need to open the Apache configuration directory (if you used the default location, it should be C:\Program Files\Apache Group\Apache2\conf) and edit httpd.conf. Then you need to add the following lines to the end of the file:

```
LoadModule php5_module c:/php/php5apache2.dll
AddType application/x-httpd-php .php
```

When you next restart your web server from the Apache monitor, the PHP extension will be loaded. To test PHP, you can create in the htdocs folder under your Apache installation location a simple script that looks like this:

```
<?php
phpinfo();
?>
```

In your web browser, if you visit http://localhost/index.php, you should see a page that gives lots of information on the PHP configuration.

Troubleshooting

If you experience installation problems, first you should check that you have followed the steps in this chapter exactly. If you continue to have difficulties, try the following websites, which may be able to provide assistance:

- http://httpd.apache.org/docs-2.0/faq/support.html

- www.php.net/manual/en/faq.build.php

INDEX